Cooks in a Hurry
Fondue Cookery

by

CAROLYN HUMPHRIES

and

CHRISTINE SMEETH

foulsham

London • New York • Toronto • Sydney

foulsham

The Publishing House, Bennetts Close,
Cippenham, Berkshire, SL1 5AP, England.

ISBN 0-572-02306-5

Printed in Great Britain by
St. Edmundsbury Press, Bury St. Edmunds, Suffolk

Contents

Introduction	4
Practicalities	5
The Basic Procedure	8
Cheese Fondues	11
Fish Fondues	28
Meat Fondues	46
Speciality Fondues	90
Vegetable Fondues	107
Sauces and Dips	118
Convenience Fondues	138
Dessert Fondues	144
Index	157

Introduction

You may have thought that having a fondue meant lots of work and effort, but it doesn't. It is just a great excuse for sitting around eating and drinking with family or friends. All the recipes in this book are quick and easy to prepare – many can even be knocked up on the spur of the moment. Even the most exotic fondues need just a little preparation and careful presentation. And all the sauces can be whipped up in minutes. This book tells you everything you need to know to have a perfect fondue party or a tasty family supper. And the great thing is, everyone does their own cooking so you don't have to spend hours slaving over a hot stove!

You may like to start by trying a cheese fondue for a simple supper on its own, or serve a sweet fondue as dessert one night. Then, when you get used to the idea of everyone getting stuck in, go the whole hog with a fondue party. You could start with a cheese fondue, followed by a fish, meat and/or vegetable one and finish off with a sensational sweet one.

Once you have tried it, you are sure to want to try it again!

Practicalities

Here are some top tips to make sure that whatever type of fondue you make, it will be an instant success.

BASIC EQUIPMENT

A traditional fondue pot has a dipping pot at the top with a candle flame or methylated spirit burner underneath. You can buy electric ones too – at a price! Earthenware or pottery pots tend to be wider and shallow which makes them ideal for cheese or sweet fondues which need constant stirring. Cast iron or stainless steel pots are more popular for hot oil or stock for meat, fish or vegetable fondues as they retain heat more efficiently. But they are interchangeable when needs be. At a push you can improvise with a heavy-based pan (like a Le Creuset) and a candle flame heated tray (the sort for keeping foot hot at the table).

If you are serving more than one fondue – perhaps a meat or vegetable fondue followed by a sweet one – why not borrow one from a friend to make the organisation easier?

For all fondues, avoid having tall-stemmed glasses on the table as they invariably get knocked over with all the leaning across to the fondue pot!

CHEESE FONDUES

• Cheese fondues can be made on the conventional cooker then transferred to the fondue burner to keep warm during serving if preferred.

• It is essential to keep it warm through the dipping time or it will set. But once the mixture is hot, the flame should be lowered immediately or it will burn and stick to the base of the pot.

• If the mixture thickens too much and forms a ball, continue to heat gently, stirring all the time over a very low heat and thin with a little more wine (or milk if not using alcohol).

• Cubes of French bread are the usual dipper but speciality breads, crackers or vegetable sticks may also be served (see individual recipes).

MEAT, FISH AND VEGETABLE FONDUES

• Use good quality oil like sunflower or corn for cooking. For extra flavour use a quarter olive, sesame or walnut oil (but this is expensive). Fill the fondue pot no more than half-full or as directed in the instructions.

• It is often easier and quicker to heat the oil or stock on the conventional cooker, then transfer it to the burner on the table to keep hot. Do make sure it is very hot before starting to cook, or the ingredients will be soggy and unpalatable.

• The oil should be bubbling, not smoking (190°C/375°F on a thermometer) or when a cube of day-old bread browns in 30 seconds.

• Have plenty of kitchen paper or paper napkins on hand for draining food and for mopping up dribbles and spills (fondue parties tend to be rather messy affairs).

• Ensure that meat or fish is very fresh or completely thawed if previously frozen.

• Make sure that pieces of meat, fish or vegetable are not too big or they will take too long to cook.

SWEET FONDUES

• As they have a high sugar content, the cooking syrup can catch and burn easily, so keep the heat low and stir frequently even during serving.

• Don't overheat chocolate, in particular, as it will turn granular if it burns.

• If choosing cake as a dipper, make sure it is not too crumbly or you'll end up with a pot full of bits!

• Choose firm fruits which will spear easily (they taste even better if chilled first) and don't cut them up too small or they will disintegrate.

The Basic Procedure

Make sure the fondue pot is centrally placed on the table so that each guest can reach it.

❶ Each guest is given a plate and two forks, usually colour coded (so they can tell which is theirs when in the pot). One fork is for dipping or cooking, one for eating. This isn't just for hygienic purposes - it's to prevent burning the mouth!

❷ For a cheese fondue, cubes of bread are handed round and each guest takes a handful (or a small bowl of bread cubes is put at each place).

❸ Guests spear a cube of bread, dip it in the hot cheese fondue, twiddle it round to stop the drips, transfer it to their place then spear it with the second fork to eat it.

❹ For a meat, fish and/or vegetable fondue, the pot of hot oil or stock is placed in the centre, each guest has the raw meat or fish and/or vegetables arranged attractively on his plate, with a small bowl of batter if necessary.

• Each guest spears a piece of food, dips it in batter if necessary, then plunges it in the hot oil to cook to their own liking. It is then transferred to a clean plate and another piece speared and plunged in the pot.

• Sauces or dips are handed around and each guest takes small spoonfuls ready to dip their cooked morsels in (OR individual tiny dishes are arranged at each place OR plates with several sections can be used to accommodate the sauces and dips).

• Plain, garlic, or herb bread is usually handed round too and the whole meal rounded off with a dressed salad to complement the main ingredients. (In some recipes, potatoes, tiny vegetables or rice are suggested where appropriate.)

❺ The sweet fondue is usually ready just to heat through and bring to the table once all the main course debris has been cleared away.

• Each guest is either handed a plate with the fruit/biscuit/cake/sweetmeat dippers arranged attractively on it OR a large platter is offered round for guests to help themselves. Then the same principle as a cheese fondue applies. Guests spear, dip, transfer and eat at their leisure.

WHAT TO DRINK

• It is traditional to serve small glasses of kirsch or schnapps and hot tea with a cheese fondue. Alternatively a dry white wine - but NEVER iced drinks.

• For a meat or fish fondue, appropriate red, white or rosé wine may be served or chilled lager or cider.

• For sweet fondues, a sweet sparkling wine goes particularly well or if it's a winter party, offer tiny glasses of peach, orange or coffee liqueur.

• The best non-alcoholic alternatives are grape juice with cheese, meat, fish or vegetable fondues. The sparkling herbal or elderflower drinks are particularly good with sweet fondues.

THE SECRETS OF SUCCESS

There are three key words to remember when planning a fondue:

Organisation
Make sure everything is ready for the final cooking before guests arrive.

Presentation
Food should be laid out attractively at individual places where appropriate or within easy access of all guests.

Informality
A relaxed atmosphere and comfortable chairs are a must as diners sit around cooking, dipping, eating and drinking for a long time!

Notes on the Recipes
• Use either metric, imperial or American measures; do not swop from one to another.

• All spoon measures are level: 15 ml = 1 tbsp; 5 ml = 1 tsp.

• Always wash, dry and peel, if necessary, fresh produce before use.

• All eggs are size 3 unless otherwise stated.

• When chopped herbs are called for, they are fresh. If substituting dried, halve the quantity as they are very pungent.

• Every recipe recommends sauces and accompaniments. These are intended as a guide only – be adventurous!

• Preparation times are approximate.

Cheese Fondues

Rich, smooth, decadent, delicious – four perfect ways to describe these wonderful concoctions.

Belgian Fondue

Serve with Cranberry Relish (see page 135) as an hors d'oeuvre or as a savoury finish to a meal instead of the usual dessert.

SERVES 4

INGREDIENTS	METRIC	IMPERIAL	AMERICAN
Butter	50 g	2 oz	1/4 cup
Plain (all-purpose) flour	75 g	3 oz	3/4 cup
Milk	600 ml	1 pint	2 1/2 cups
Salt and freshly ground black pepper			
Pinch of cayenne			
Grated nutmeg	2.5 ml	1/2 tsp	1/2 tsp
Egg yolks	5	5	5
Parmesan cheese, grated	50 g	2 oz	1/2 cup
Egg, beaten	1	1	1
Breadcrumbs	30 ml	2 tbsp	2 tbsp
Oil for fondue cooking			

METHOD

❶ Melt the butter in a saucepan and stir in two-thirds of the flour. Gradually stir in the milk until the mixture is boiling.

❷ Season with the salt, pepper, cayenne and nutmeg. Beat in the eggs and Parmesan cheese.

❸ Pour the mixture into a flat tin (pan) and allow to cool and set.

❹ Cut the savoury into small rounds with a biscuit (cookie) cutter and coat with the remaining flour.

5 Place the beaten egg and breadcrumbs on separate plates. Dip each savoury into egg, then breadcrumbs and cook in hot oil until brown.

Preparation time: 10 minutes plus cooling

Simple Gruyère Fondue

A quick and easy method and particularly suitable for those who prefer their fondues without alcohol.

SERVES 6

INGREDIENTS	METRIC	IMPERIAL	AMERICAN
Butter	25 g	1 oz	2 tbsp
Plain (all-purpose) flour	25 g	1 oz	1/4 cup
Milk	450 ml	3/4 pt	2 cups
Gruyère (Swiss) cheese, grated	450 g	1 lb	4 cups
Grated nutmeg	5 ml	1 tsp	1 tsp
Salt and freshly ground black pepper			

METHOD

1 Light the flame under a fondue pot and warm the dish.

2 Melt the butter and add the flour, stirring continuously.

3 Add the milk, a little at a time until the sauce begins to thicken and gradually blend in the cheese. Season with the nutmeg, salt and pepper.

Preparation time: 10 minutes

Camembert and Calvados

Crisp apples, cored, peeled and cut into chunks should be prepared at the last moment to ensure that they do not go brown. Put the apple chunks in a bowl and coat with lemon juice. Pat dry on kitchen paper and serve.

SERVES 3–4

INGREDIENTS	METRIC	IMPERIAL	AMERICAN
Garlic clove	*¹/₂*	*¹/₂*	*¹/₂*
Dry white wine	*150 ml*	*¹/₄ pt*	*²/₃ cup*
Single (light) cream	*150 ml*	*¹/₄ pt*	*²/₃ cup*
Camembert cheese,			
cubed	*275 g*	*10 oz*	*2¹/₂ cups*
Cornflour (cornstarch)	*15 ml*	*1 tbsp*	*1 tbsp*
Calvados	*45 ml*	*3 tbsp*	*3 tbsp*

METHOD

❶ Rub the inside of a fondue pot with cut garlic and pour in the wine. Heat until bubbling and turn the heat to very low.

❷ Pour in the cream and add the cheese cubes, stirring all the time until melted.

❸ Blend the cornflour with the Calvados. Stir into the cheese mixture and cook for 2 minutes, stirring.

❹ Serve with chunks of crispy apples and cold cooked sausages.

Preparation time: 10 minutes

Fondue Italienne

Serve with olives, thick chunks of red, green and yellow pepper and rolls of salami sausage.

SERVES 6

INGREDIENTS	METRIC	IMPERIAL	AMERICAN
Garlic clove	*¹/₂*	*¹/₂*	*¹/₂*
Milk	*300 ml*	*¹/₂ pt*	*1¹/₄ cups*
Mozzarella cheese,			
* grated*	*350 g*	*12 oz*	*3 cups*
Cheddar cheese, grated	*175 g*	*6 oz*	*1¹/₂ cups*
Parmesan cheese, freshly			
* grated*	*50 g*	*2 oz*	*¹/₂ cup*
Cornflour (cornstarch)	*10 ml*	*2 tbsp*	*2 tbsp*
Dry white wine	*45 ml*	*3 tbsp*	*3 tbsp*
Finely chopped basil	*5 ml*	*1 tsp*	*1 tsp*

METHOD

❶ Rub the inside of a fondue pot with the cut side of the garlic clove.

❷ Add the milk to the fondue pot and heat until almost boiling. Lower the heat.

❸ Stir in the cheeses and continue to heat until melted.

❹ Blend the cornflour with the wine and stir into the cheese mixture. Cook for 2–3 minutes until the fondue is creamy, stirring all the time. Blend in the chopped basil.

Preparation time: 10 minutes

Curried Fondue

Still cheese, but with the addition of curry paste which can be adapted to suit the palate. Serve with pieces of naan bread and a Cucumber and Mint Sauce (see page 138).

SERVES 4-6

INGREDIENTS	METRIC	IMPERIAL	AMERICAN
Garlic clove	¹/₂	¹/₂	¹/₂
White wine	175 ml	6 fl oz	³/₄ cup
Lemon juice	5 ml	1 tsp	1 tsp
Hot curry paste	5 ml	1 tsp	1 tsp
Cheddar cheese, grated	225 g	8 oz	2 cups
Gruyère (Swiss) cheese, grated	175 g	6 oz	1¹/₂ cups
Cornflour (cornstarch)	10 ml	2 tsp	2 tsp
Sweet sherry or port	30 ml	2 tbsp	2 tbsp

METHOD

❶ Rub the inside of a fondue pot with the cut clove of garlic.

❷ Pour in the wine and lemon juice and heat until boiling. Reduce the heat to low and stir in the curry paste.

❸ Add the grated cheeses and continue to heat, stirring frequently.

❹ Blend the cornflour with the sherry or port and pour into the mixture.

❺ Cook for 3–4 minutes until the mixture thickens. Do not allow the fondue to boil.

Preparation time: 10 minutes

Swiss Fondue

Chunks of crusty bread are the usual accompaniment to this fondue. But for a change, try cubes of brioche alternated with crisp bread sticks.

SERVES 4

INGREDIENTS	METRIC	IMPERIAL	AMERICAN
Butter	*15 g*	*¹/₂ oz*	*1 tbsp*
Gruyère (Swiss) cheese,			
grated	*450 g*	*1 lb*	*4 cups*
Dry white wine	*375 ml*	*13 fl oz*	*1¹/₂ cups*
Kirsch	*60 ml*	*4 tbsp*	*4 tbsp*
Dry mustard	*5 ml*	*1 tsp*	*1 tsp*
Pinch of grated nutmeg			

METHOD

1 Melt the butter in a fondue pot.

2 Add the cheese and stir until melting.

3 Gradually add the wine, stirring all the time.

4 Blend a little of the kirsch with the mustard powder and stir into the pot with the remaining kirsch and nutmeg.

5 When smooth and gently bubbling, serve.

Preparation time: 10 minutes

Golden Camemberts

Said to have been created around 1790, Camembert comes from Normandy but only became famous in the late 1800s. The soft creamy-yellow centre should be at the peak of ripeness for this recipe. It is essential to use small Chinese wire strainers to lift the cheese portions in and out of the oil as fondue forks will pierce the crust and the cheese will ooze through.

SERVES 4

INGREDIENTS	METRIC	IMPERIAL	AMERICAN
Small round Camembert cheese	*1*	*1*	*1*
Eggs, beaten	*2*	*2*	*2*
Dried breadcrumbs	*100 g*	*4 oz*	*1 cup*
Chopped parsley	*45 ml*	*3 tbsp*	*3 tbsp*
Oil for fondue cooking			

METHOD

❶ Cut the Camembert into small, triangular size portions and freeze for 40 minutes.

❷ Put the beaten eggs in a flat dish and dip each cheese portion in the egg and then in the breadcrumbs. Set aside.

❸ Mix the remaining breadcrumbs and the parsley together.

❹ Dip the portions of cheese again in the egg and breadcrumb and herb mix. Chill until required.

5 Pour the oil into a fondue pot and heat until the oil is bubbling. Each person dips their Camembert portions into the oil with the aid of a small strainer and cooks them until golden. Serve with Cranberry Relish (see page 135) and a fresh, chopped salad.

Preparation time: 10 minutes plus chilling

Worcestershire Fondue

Serve with small, cooked sausages, chunks of apple and cubes of bread.

SERVES 4

INGREDIENTS	METRIC	IMPERIAL	AMERICAN
Milk	*250 ml*	*8 fl oz*	*1 cup*
Smoked cheese, grated	*350 g*	*12 oz*	*3 cups*
Cornflour (cornstarch)	*20 ml*	*4 tsp*	*4 tsp*
Horseradish sauce	*10 ml*	*2 tsp*	*2 tsp*
Made mustard	*5 ml*	*1 tsp*	*1 tsp*
Worcestershire sauce	*10 ml*	*2 tsp*	*2 tsp*

METHOD

1 Pour the milk into the fondue pot and heat until boiling.

2 Add the cheese and stir over a low heat until smooth.

3 Blend the cornflour with the horseradish sauce, mustard and the Worcestershire sauce and mix into the fondue. Cook for 2–3 minutes, stirring until thickened. Serve.

Preparation time: 10 minutes

A Romantic Fondue

Light the fire, draw the curtains and slip into something more comfortable for this delicious fondue experience. French bread is all that's needed to accompany it.

SERVES 2

INGREDIENTS	METRIC	IMPERIAL	AMERICAN
Garlic clove, cut in half	1	1	1
Dry white wine	750 ml	1¼ pts	3 cups
Emmental (Swiss) cheese, grated	175 g	6 oz	1½ cups
Leerdammer cheese, grated	175 g	6 oz	1½ cups
Cornflour (cornstarch)	10 ml	2 tsp	2 tsp
Kirsch	60 ml	4 tbsp	4 tbsp
Salt and freshly ground black pepper			
To serve			
Lots of chilled dry white wine and a small glass of kirsch each			

METHOD

❶ Rub the inside of a fondue pot with the garlic then discard.

❷ Add the wine and heat until it bubbles.

❸ Gradually add the cheese, stirring all the time until melted into the wine.

❹ Blend the cornflour with the kirsch and stir in
Cook until gently simmering then reduce hea
with chilled white wine. Halfway through the meal, drink
half the glass of kirsch. Drink the rest at the end.

Preparation time: 10 minutes

Ploughman's Fondue

Serve with crusty farmhouse bread and pickled onions.

SERVES 4

INGREDIENTS	METRIC	IMPERIAL	AMERICAN
Mature Cheddar cheese,			
grated	*225 g*	*8 oz*	*2 cups*
Butter, cut in cubes	*100 g*	*4 oz*	*1/2 cup*
Eggs, beaten	*6*	*6*	*6*
Paprika	*2.5 ml*	*1/2 tsp*	*1/2 tsp*
Pinch of cayenne			
Salt and freshly ground			
black pepper			

METHOD

❶ Put the cheese and butter in a fondue pot with the eggs.

❷ Cook over a gently heat, stirring constantly until the
mixture is smooth and thick. DO NOT BOIL or the
mixture will scramble.

❸ Turn the heat as low as possible, season with paprika,
cayenne, salt and pepper and serve.

Preparation time: 10 minutes

Italian Pizza Fondue

Serve with plain ciabatta bread or one flavoured with olives.

SERVES 4

INGREDIENTS	METRIC	IMPERIAL	AMERICAN
Butter	15 g	1/2 oz	1 tbsp
Button mushrooms, sliced	50 g	2 oz	1 cup
Garlic clove, crushed	1 small	1 small	1 small
Can tomatoes, sieved	225 g	8 oz	small can
Fontina cheese, grated	225 g	8 oz	2 cups
Cornflour (cornstarch)	15 ml	1 tbsp	1 tbsp
Can evaporated milk	170 g	6 3/4 oz	small can
Onion salt	2.5 ml	1/2 tsp	1/2 tsp
Dried oregano	2.5 ml	1/2 tsp	1/2 tsp

METHOD

1 Melt the butter in the fondue pot. Add the mushrooms and garlic and cook for 2 minutes, stirring.

2 Add the tomatoes and bring to the boil.

3 Mix the cheese and cornflour together. Stir into the tomato mixture until melted.

4 Gradually stir in the evaporated milk then season with the onion salt and oregano.

5 When gently bubbling, serve.

Preparation time: 10 minutes

Caerphilly Fondue

Serve with cubes of soda bread and cold, cooked lamb, cut into bite-sized chunks.

SERVES 4

INGREDIENTS	METRIC	IMPERIAL	AMERICAN
Butter	*25 g*	*1 oz*	*2 tbsp*
Water	*30 ml*	*2 tbsp*	*2 tbsp*
Leeks, trimmed and finely chopped	*100 g*	*4 oz*	*1 cup*
Celery sticks, finely chopped	*2*	*2*	*2*
Light ale	*300 ml*	*¹/₂ pt*	*1¹/₄ cups*
Cornflour (cornstarch)	*15 ml*	*1 tbsp*	*1 tbsp*
Caerphilly cheese, cubed	*275 g*	*10 oz*	*2¹/₂ cups*
Freshly ground black pepper			

METHOD

❶ Heat the butter in a frying pan (skillet). Add the water, leeks and celery and cook for 2 minutes.

❷ Pour in the light ale, cover, lower the heat and cook gently for 8–10 minutes until the vegetables are tender.

❸ Strain a little of the stock from the pan into a cup and blend with the cornflour. Stir into the vegetables and cook for 1 minute until thickened, stirring all the time.

❹ Place in a fondue pot and gradually add the cheese. Cook until melted, stirring. Season with the pepper.

Preparation time: 15 minutes

Bianco Fondue

Serve stuffed olives and breadsticks with this fragrant cheese fondue.

SERVES 4

INGREDIENTS	METRIC	IMPERIAL	AMERICAN
Bianco vermouth	250 ml	8 fl oz	1 cup
Fontina cheese, grated	225 g	8 oz	2 cups
Leerdammer cheese, grated	225 g	8 oz	2 cups
Cornflour (cornstarch)	30 ml	2 tbsp	2 tbsp
Egg yolks	2	2	2
Medium dry white wine	250 ml	8 fl oz	1 cup
Few drops of Tabasco sauce			
Freshly ground black pepper			

METHOD

❶ Put the vermouth in the fondue pot and heat gently.

❷ Mix the cheeses with the cornflour. Gradually stir into the pot.

❸ When melted, beat the egg yolks with the wine and stir into the pot. Continue stirring until the mixture begins to bubble.

❹ Season with the Tabasco sauce and pepper to taste.

Preparation time: 10 minutes

Dutch Fondue

Gin adds an interesting fragrance and piquancy to this fondue. Serve with 'dippers' of raw vegetables and Dutch crispbake crackers.

SERVES 4–6

INGREDIENTS	METRIC	IMPERIAL	AMERICAN
Garlic clove	*¹/₂*	*¹/₂*	*¹/₂*
Milk	*250 ml*	*8 fl oz*	*1 cup*
Gouda cheese, grated	*225 g*	*8 oz*	*2 cups*
Edam cheese, grated	*225 g*	*8 oz*	*2 cups*
Grated nutmeg	*5 ml*	*1 tsp*	*1 tsp*
Cornflour (cornstarch)	*15 ml*	*1 tbsp*	*1 tbsp*
Gin	*30 ml*	*2 tbsp*	*2 tbsp*
Freshly ground black pepper			

METHOD

❶ Rub the inside of a fondue pot with the cut side of the garlic then discard.

❷ Add the milk and heat until boiling. Gradually stir in the cheese.

❸ Lower the heat and stir in the nutmeg.

❹ Blend the cornflour with the gin and stir into the cheese mixture. Season with the pepper and cook for 2–3 minutes, stirring until thickened.

Preparation time: 10 minutes

Rich Geneva Convention

Croûtes (thick pieces of fried bread) are often served with this luxurious fondue, but onion and/or sun-dried tomato bread complements it perfectly.

SERVES 4

INGREDIENTS	METRIC	IMPERIAL	AMERICAN
Gruyère (Swiss) cheese, grated	225 g	8 oz	2 cups
Egg yolks	8	8	8
Grated nutmeg	1.5 g	1/4 tsp	1/4 tsp
Butter, cut in cubes	100 g	4 oz	1/2 cup
Single (light) cream	150 ml	1/4 pt	2/3 cup
Salt and freshly ground black pepper			

METHOD

❶ Beat the cheese and egg yolks together in a fondue pot.

❷ Add the nutmeg then stir over a gentle heat until the cheese melts. DO NOT BOIL.

❸ Add the butter, piece by piece, stirring until the mixture thickens and absorbs it.

❹ Stir in the cream and heat through. Season to taste.

Preparation time: 10 minutes

Cheese and Vegetable Fondue

This recipe makes a lovely change from the richer cheese fondues. It is best made on top of the stove then transferred to the table. Serve with button mushrooms, cherry tomatoes, strips of green, red and yellow (bell) peppers and baby corn cobs for dipping.

SERVES 4

INGREDIENTS	METRIC	IMPERIAL	AMERICAN
Butter	50 g	2 oz	$^1/_4$ cup
Plain (all-purpose) flour	30 ml	2 tbsp	2 tbsp
Dry white wine	375 ml	13 fl oz	$1^1/_2$ cups
Emmental (Swiss) cheese, grated	100 g	4 oz	1 cup
Parmesan cheese, grated	100 g	4 oz	1 cup
Thick plain yoghurt	45 ml	3 tbsp	3 tbsp
Dried basil	2.5 ml	$^1/_2$ tsp	$^1/_2$ tsp
Freshly ground black pepper			

METHOD

❶ Melt the butter in a fondue pot. Add the flour and cook for 1 minute stirring.

❷ Gradually whisk in the wine and bring to the boil, whisking until smooth and thickened.

❸ Mix the cheeses together then add a handful at a time, stirring until melted.

❹ Stir in the yoghurt and basil. Season with pepper and bring to the table.

Preparation time: 10 minutes

Fish Fondues

Whether you choose to serve a completely fish fondue or one that is a combination of seafood and meat, they make mouthwatering meals for any occasion. Some recipes here are for simple family suppers, others for more elegant affairs.

Seafood Fondue

Serve with a Red Pepper Sauce (see page 134) and Cucumber and Mint Sauce (see page 138).

SERVES 6

INGREDIENTS	METRIC	IMPERIAL	AMERICAN
Plaice fillets, skinned and boned	2	2	2
Halibut, skinned and boned	225 g	8 oz	$^1/_2$ lb
Cod, skinned and boned	225 g	8 oz	$^1/_2$ lb
Large peeled prawns (jumbo shrimp)	225 g	8 oz	2 cups
Shelled mussels	175 g	6 oz	$1^1/_2$ cups
Juice of 2 lemons			
Oyster sauce	5 ml	1 tsp	1 tsp
Cornflour (cornstarch)	30 ml	2 tbsp	2 tbsp
Oil for fondue cooking			

METHOD

❶ Place the fish in a large bowl and sprinkle over the lemon juice and oyster sauce. Cover and chill for 20 minutes.

❷ Remove from the bowl and dust with cornflour. Arrange on a serving plate.

❸ Heat the oil in a fondue pot until bubbling and serve.

Preparation time: 15 minutes plus chilling

Bagna Cauda

This wonderful speciality needs nothing more than some warm ciabatta bread or crisp bread sticks.

SERVES 4

INGREDIENTS	METRIC	IMPERIAL	AMERICAN
Bulb of Florence fennel, trimmed and cut in strips	1	1	1
Carrots, cut in strips	2	2	2
Red (bell) pepper, cut in strips	1	1	1
Green or yellow (bell) pepper, cut in strips	1	1	1
Celery sticks, cut in strips	2	2	2
Large cucumber, cut in strips	1/4	1/4	1/4
Olive oil	150 ml	1/4 pt	2/3 cup
Butter	50 g	2 oz	1/4 cup
Garlic cloves, crushed	3	3	3
Cans anchovies	2 x 50 g	2 x 2 oz	2 small cans

METHOD

❶ Chill the vegetables for at least 1 hour.

❷ Put the oil, butter and garlic in a fondue pot or a saucepan.

❸ Drain the anchovy oil into the pan. Chop the fish finely and add.

❹ Simmer gently for 5 minutes. Transfer to a fondue pot if necessary and place on the table.

❺ Guests dip cold vegetables into the hot fishy oil, stirring up the sediment every time.

Preparation time: 15 minutes plus chilling

Sole and Sherry Fondue

This is equally good using plaice fillets instead of sole.

SERVES 4–6

INGREDIENTS	METRIC	IMPERIAL	AMERICAN
Lemon sole fillets, skinned	3	3	3
Fish stock	900 ml	1½ pts	3¾ cups
Fresh root ginger, sliced	10 ml	2 tsp	2 tsp
Dry sherry	45 ml	3 tbsp	3 tbsp
Chopped coriander (cilantro)	15 ml	1 tbsp	1 tbsp

METHOD

❶ Cut the sole fillets into thin strips and arrange on a dish.

❷ Put the fish stock in a fondue pot or a saucepan with the ginger and simmer for 10 minutes. Add the sherry and coriander. Simmer for 5 minutes. Transfer to a fondue pot if necessary and place on the table.

❸ Each person cooks their own fish using Chinese wire strainers.

Preparation time: 20 minutes

Filled Filo Parcels

The parcels are cooked in hot oil in the fondue pot, using Chinese wire strainers for cooking and lifting the fish parcels from the hot oil.

SERVES 6

INGREDIENTS	METRIC	IMPERIAL	AMERICAN
Large peeled prawns			
(jumbo shrimp)	175 g	6 oz	1¹/₂ cups
Button mushrooms,			
chopped	100 g	4 oz	2 cups
Oyster sauce	10 ml	2 tsp	2 tsp
Lemon juice	10 ml	2 tsp	2 tsp
Freshly ground black pepper			
Butter	50 g	2 oz	¹/₄ cup
Filo pastry (paste)	4 sheets	4 sheets	4 sheets
Oil for fondue cooking			

METHOD

❶ In a bowl, mix the peeled prawns and chopped mushrooms.

❷ Sprinkle over the oyster sauce and lemon juice. Season with the pepper and leave to marinate for 15–30 minutes.

❸ Melt the butter in a saucepan.

❹ Cut the pastry into 18 15 cm/6 in squares. Brush with melted butter. Place 15 ml/1 tbsp prawn and mushroom mix at one end of each square. Fold over each side, then roll up the parcel so that it resembles a spring roll. Set aside on a decorative plate until needed.

❺ Heat the oil in a fondue pot until bubbling. Serve.

Preparation time: 15 minutes plus marinating

Spicy Prawns

Serve with Rouille, (page 123), Peppercorn Sauce (page 130) and Garlic Sauce (page 133).

SERVES 4

INGREDIENTS	METRIC	IMPERIAL	AMERICAN
King prawns (jumbo shrimp)	750 g	$1^1/_2$ lb	$1^1/_2$ lb
Sunflower oil	30 ml	2 tbsp	2 tbsp
Paprika	5 ml	1 tsp	1 tsp
Ground ginger	2.5 ml	$^1/_2$ tsp	$^1/_2$ tsp
Lemon juice	15 ml	1 tbsp	1 tbsp
Dry white wine	60 ml	4 tbsp	4 tbsp
Oil for fondue cooking			

METHOD

❶ Peel the prawns and put into a bowl. Add the oil, paprika, ginger, lemon juice and wine and mix well.

❷ Cover the prawns with cling film (self-cling plastic wrap) and allow to marinate for 1 hour in the fridge. Arrange on serving plates.

❸ Heat the oil in a fondue pot until bubbling and serve.

Preparation time: 10 minutes plus marinating

Plaice Goujons

Serve with chunky cut vegetables, Sweet Spicy Sauce (page 136), tartare sauce and lemon wedges.

SERVES 4

INGREDIENTS	METRIC	IMPERIAL	AMERICAN
Plain (all-purpose) flour	45 ml	3 tbsp	3 tbsp
Chopped mixed herbs	15 ml	1 tbsp	1 tbsp
Salt and freshly ground black pepper			
Plaice fillets, skinned	4	4	4
Eggs, beaten	3	3	3
Dried breadcrumbs	100 g	4 oz	1 cup
Oil for fondue cooking			

METHOD

❶ Mix the flour, herbs, salt and pepper in a shallow dish.

❷ Cut the plaice fillets into long strips about 1 cm/¹/₂ in wide and dust each piece with the seasoned flour.

❸ Place the beaten eggs in a shallow dish and dip each piece of fish in the mixture. Coat with the breadcrumbs.

❹ Repeat the egg and breadcrumbs process and chill.

❺ Heat the oil in a fondue pot until bubbling. Each person spears a piece of fish and fries it until the breadcrumbs are golden brown.

Preparation time: 10 minutes plus chilling

Fish Balls

Serve with Cucumber and Mint Sauce (page 138), tartare sauce and Caviar Sauce (page 125).

SERVES 6

INGREDIENTS	METRIC	IMPERIAL	AMERICAN
White fish, skinned and boned	*750 g*	*1¹/₂ lb*	*1¹/₂ lb*
Onion, chopped	*1*	*1*	*1*
Fine matzo meal	*100 g*	*4 oz*	*1 cup*
Fresh breadcrumbs	*50 g*	*2 oz*	*1 cup*
Chopped parsley	*30 ml*	*2 tbsp*	*2 tbsp*
Salt and freshly ground black pepper			
Eggs, beaten	*2*	*2*	*2*
Oil for fondue cooking			

METHOD

① Place the fish and onion in a food processor and blend for 1 minute.

② Add the matzo meal, breadcrumbs, parsley and salt and pepper. Add the beaten eggs and blend until it is well mixed.

③ Form the mixture into balls and chill for 1 hour.

④ Heat the oil in a fondue pot until bubbling. Each person spears a fish ball with a fondue fork and cooks it in hot oil until golden.

Preparation time: 15 minutes plus chilling

Surf 'n' Turf Fondue

This lovely combination of fish and meat is simmered in a wine flavoured stock. Serve with Dill Cream (page 126), horseradish sauce, Hot Curry Sauce (page 132), Mustard Sauce (page 131) and Peppercorn Sauce (page 130).

SERVES 4

INGREDIENTS	METRIC	IMPERIAL	AMERICAN
Halibut or other flat fish			
fillet, cut in bite-sized			
pieces	*225 g*	*8 oz*	*2 cups*
Fillet steak, cubed	*225 g*	*8 oz*	*2 cups*
Lamb's kidneys, quartered			
and cored	*4*	*4*	*4*
Juice of 1 lemon			
Few drops of Worcestershire			
sauce			
Carrots, sliced	*4*	*4*	*4*
Celery stick, sliced	*1*	*1*	*1*
Small leek, sliced	*1*	*1*	*1*
Glass dry white wine	*1*	*1*	*1*
Cider vinegar	*120 ml*	*4 fl oz*	*¹/₂ cup*
Beef stock	*750 ml*	*1¹/₄ pts*	*3 cups*
Onion, studded with 3			
cloves	*1*	*1*	*1*
Sprig of thyme			
Freshly ground black pepper			

METHOD

❶ Put the fish and meat in a dish and sprinkle with the lemon juice and Worcestershire sauce.

❷ Cook the carrots, celery and leek in boiling water for 3 minutes, drain and rinse with cold water. Drain again.

❸ Arrange the fish and meat attractively on serving plates with the blanched vegetables.

❹ Put the wine, vinegar and stock in a fondue pot with the studded onion and the thyme. Simmer for at least 5 minutes then remove the onion and herbs.

❺ Season lightly with pepper then serve.

Preparation time: 20 minutes

Creamy Champagne and Seafood Fondue

The most magnificent combination of flavours makes this fondue for a special occasion indeed! Serve with Caviar Sauce (page 125), Herb Cream (page 127) and Cocktail Sauce (page 124).

SERVES 4

INGREDIENTS	METRIC	IMPERIAL	AMERICAN
Monkfish, cubed	100 g	4 oz	1 cup
Smoked trout fillets, skinned and cut in thin strips	2	2	2
Fillet steak, cut in thin strips	100 g	4 oz	1 cup
Raw smoked gammon, cubed	100 g	4 oz	1 cup
Glass dry Champagne (or sparkling wine)	1	1	1
Beef stock	250 ml	8 fl oz	1 cup
Whipping cream	150 ml	1/4 pt	2/3 cup
Grated Parmesan cheese	15 ml	1 tbsp	1 tbsp
Sprig of tarragon			
Pinch of caster (superfine) sugar			
Pinch of grated nutmeg			
Freshly ground black pepper			

METHOD

❶ Arrange the fish and meat on serving plates.

❷ Put the Champagne into a fondue pot with the stock, cream, Parmesan, herbs and sugar. Bring to the boil and leave to stand for 5 minutes.

❸ Remove the sprig of tarragon and add the nutmeg and a little pepper. Heat through again and serve when bubbling gently.

Preparation time: 15 minutes

Cornish Crab Fondue

Serve this gorgeous concoction with lots of crusty bread and glasses of chilled dry sherry then follow with a crisp salad.

SERVES 4

INGREDIENTS	METRIC	IMPERIAL	AMERICAN
Can Cornish crab soup	425 g	15 oz	1 large can
Milk	1/2 soup can	1/2 soup can	1/2 soup can
Cheddar cheese, grated	50 g	2 oz	1/2 cup
Can crab meat	170 g	6 oz	1 small can
Good pinch of cayenne			
Sherry	30 ml	2 tbsp	2 tbsp

METHOD

❶ Put the soup in a fondue pot with the milk. Add the cheese and heat through until it melts. Stir in the remaining ingredients, heat through and serve.

Preparation time: 5 minutes

Frito Misto Di Mare Fondue

A selection of fish, fried to a golden crispness then served with tartare sauce, Garlic Sauce (page 133), Cheese and Onion Sauce (page 139) and lemon wedges.

SERVES 4

INGREDIENTS	METRIC	IMPERIAL	AMERICAN
Cod or haddock fillet, skinned and cut in cubes	*175 g*	*6 oz*	*1¹/₂ cups*
Squid, cut in rings	*175 g*	*6 oz*	*1¹/₂ cups*
Monkfish, cubed or scampi	*175 g*	*6 oz*	*1¹/₂ cups*
Whitebait	*100 g*	*4 oz*	*1 cup*
Cornflour (cornstarch) for dusting			
For the batter			
Plain (all-purpose) flour	*200 g*	*7 oz*	*1³/₄ cups*
Pinch of salt			
Water	*300 ml*	*¹/₂ pt*	*1¹/₄ cups*
Olive oil	*10 ml*	*2 tsp*	*2 tsp*
Eggs, separated	*2*	*2*	*2*
Oil for fondue cooking			

METHOD

❶ Arrange the fish on serving plates and dust with cornflour.

❷ Put the flour and salt in a bowl. Beat in the water, oil and egg yolks.

❸ Whisk the whites until stiff and fold in with a metal spoon. Pour into 4 individual bowls.

❹ Heat the oil in a fondue pot until bubbling then guests dip pieces of fish in the batter and fry until crisp and golden.

Preparation time: 15 minutes

THE NO-EFFORT FRITO MISTO

Use ready battered or crumbed scampi, squid and plaice goujons and serve with lemon wedges, tartare sauce, horseradish cream and a selection of cheese or mayonnaise-based dips.

Bretonne Fondue

Brittany is famous for its shellfish and this is a delicious way of serving it, combined with a little veal or pork fillet. Serve with Dill Cream (page 126), Garlic Sauce (page 133), Caviar Sauce (page 125) and Cocktail Sauce (page 124).

SERVES 4

INGREDIENTS	METRIC	IMPERIAL	AMERICAN
Large peeled prawns			
(jumbo shrimp)	*175 g*	*6 oz*	*1¹/₂ cups*
Shelled mussels	*175 g*	*6 oz*	*1¹/₂ cups*
Veal fillet, cubed	*175 g*	*6 oz*	*1¹/₂ cups*
Juice of 2 lemons			
Worcestershire sauce			
Salt and freshly ground			
black pepper			
Brandy	*5 ml*	*1 tsp*	*1 tsp*
Garlic cloves, chopped	*2*	*2*	*2*
Chopped mixed herbs	*60 ml*	*4 tbsp*	*4 tbsp*
Cornflour (cornstarch)	*30 ml*	*2 tbsp*	*2 tbsp*
Oil for fondue cooking			

METHOD

❶ Put the shellfish and veal in a bowl.

❷ Add all the ingredients except the cornflour and the oil and toss well. Chill for 10 minutes.

❸ Remove from the dish, toss in cornflour and arrange on serving plates.

❹ Heat the oil in a fondue pot until bubbling and serve.

Preparation time: 15 minutes plus chilling

Bouillabaisse Fondue

When you've cooked all the fish, add 15–30 ml/1–2 tbsp brandy to the stock and ladle into soup bowls. Serve the fondue with Rouille (page 123), Fines Herbes Sauce (page 129) and lots of crusty French bread.

SERVES 4

INGREDIENTS	METRIC	IMPERIAL	AMERICAN
Monkfish, cubed	225 g	8 oz	2 cups
Large peeled prawns (jumbo shrimp)	175 g	6 oz	1½ cups
Shelled mussels or oysters	175 g	6 oz	1½ cups
Lemon wedges			
Parsley sprigs			
Fish stock	1.2 L	2 pts	5 cups
Small onion, peeled	1	1	1
Bouquet garni sachet	1	1	1
Freshly ground black pepper			

METHOD

❶ Arrange the fish attractively on serving plates with the lemon wedges and parsley sprigs.

❷ Simmer the stock in a fondue pot with the onion and bouquet garni for 10 minutes then remove the onion and bouquet garni.

❸ Season with a little pepper before serving.

Preparation time: 15 minutes

Crab Stick and Artichoke Fondue

Serve this simple but exquisite fondue with Rouille (page 123).

SERVES 4

INGREDIENTS	METRIC	IMPERIAL	AMERICAN
Crab sticks, cut in four	12	12	12
Cans artichoke hearts, drained, dried and cut in bite-sized pieces	2 × 400 g	2 × 14 oz	2 large cans
Cornflour (cornstarch) for dusting			
Salt and freshly ground black pepper			
Oil for fondue cooking			

METHOD

❶ Put the crab sticks and artichoke hearts into two bowls. Sprinkle liberally with cornflour and a little salt and pepper and toss well.

❷ Arrange on serving plates.

❸ Heat the oil in a fondue pot until bubbling. Serve.

Preparation time: 5 minutes

Caribbean Fondue

Serve with Garlic Sauce (page 133), Whipped Pineapple Sauce (page 121) and Sweet Spicy Sauce (page 136).
Note: The peanut sauce given in the Indonesian Kebab Fondue (page 96) would also go well with this.

SERVES 4

INGREDIENTS	METRIC	IMPERIAL	AMERICAN
Plaice goujons in			
breadcrumbs	*225 g*	*8 oz*	*¹/₂ lb*
Chicken fingers in			
breadcrumbs	*225 g*	*8 oz*	*¹/₂ lb*
Almost-ripe bananas, cut			
in 2.5 cm/1 in pieces	*4*	*4*	*4*
Lemon juice			
Button mushrooms	*100 g*	*4 oz*	*1 cup*
Oil for fondue cooking			

METHOD

❶ Arrange the fish and chicken on serving plates.

❷ Toss the bananas in lemon juice to prevent them browning then add to the plates with the mushrooms.

❸ Heat the oil in a fondue pot until bubbling and serve.

Preparation time: 10 minutes

Meat Fondues

Even in ancient times, people enjoyed sitting around, skewering pieces of meat and cooking them communally over a fire. But meat fondues are civilisation personified – good company, good wine and fine meats cooked just the way you like them!

This section is divided into fondues cooked in oil (pages 46-69) and fondues cooked in stock (pages 70-89).

SIZZLING IN OIL FONDUES

Always remind your guests to transfer the meat from the cooking fork to their plates and eat with the other fork or there will be lots of burned tongues and lips!

Sausage Savouries

Serve with a Mustard Sauce (page 131) and Cheese and Onion Sauce (page 139).

SERVES 4

INGREDIENTS	METRIC	IMPERIAL	AMERICAN
Pork sausagemeat	450 g	1 lb	1 lb
Onion, finely chopped	1	1	1
Parmesan cheese, grated	75 g	3 oz	³/₄ cup
Made English mustard	5 ml	1 tsp	1 tsp
Chopped oregano	15 ml	1 tbsp	1 tbsp
Fresh breadcrumbs	50 g	2 oz	1 cup
Salt and freshly ground black pepper			
Eggs, beaten	2	2	2
Dried breadcrumbs	100 g	4 oz	1 cup
Oil for fondue cooking			

METHOD

❶ Break the sausagemeat into pieces and fry with the onion until lightly brown. Turn into a bowl.

❷ Add the Parmesan cheese, mustard, oregano and fresh breadcrumbs, season and mix well.

❸ Form into 16 small balls. Dip each sausage ball in beaten egg and coat with the dried breadcrumbs. Repeat this process again then place on a serving dish. Chill until required.

❹ Heat the oil in a fondue pot until bubbling. Serve.

Preparation time: 15 minutes

Farmer's Fondue

This is a fun fondue but make sure you let the ribs cool before picking them up in the fingers and dipping them in Peppercorn Sauce (page 130), Chinese Garlic Sauce (page 128) and Sweet Spicy Sauce (page 136). Serve with a dish of mixed pickles too.

SERVES 4

INGREDIENTS	METRIC	IMPERIAL	AMERICAN
Pork spare ribs	1 kg	2¹/₄ lb	2¹/₄ lb
Sunflower oil	120 ml	4 fl oz	¹/₂ cup
Light ale	120 ml	4 fl oz	¹/₂ cup
Tomato ketchup (catsup)	150 ml	¹/₄ pt	²/₃ cup
Curry powder or paste	15 ml	1 tbsp	1 tbsp
Green peppercorns (optional)	10 ml	2 tsp	2 tsp
Red or green chilli, seeded and chopped	1	1	1
Garlic cloves, chopped	2	2	2
Black treacle (molasses) or golden (light corn) syrup	20 ml	4 tsp	4 tsp
Wine vinegar	20 ml	4 tsp	4 tsp
Paprika	5 ml	1 tsp	1 tsp
Dried mixed herbs	5 ml	1 tsp	1 tsp
Oil for fondue cooking			

METHOD

❶ Chop the ribs into pieces (or ask your butcher to do so).

❷ Blend the remaining ingredients together and pour over ribs. Cover and leave to marinate in the fridge for at least 5 hours, turning several times.

❸ Arrange on serving plates. Heat the oil in a fondue pot until bubbling and serve.

Preparation time: 15 minutes plus marinating

Pork Satay

Serve this with the peanut sauce given with Indonesian Kebab Fondue (see page 96), Sweet Spicy Sauce (page 136) and Cucumber and Mint Sauce (see page 138).

SERVES 6

INGREDIENTS	METRIC	IMPERIAL	AMERICAN
Ground coriander (cilantro)	5 ml	1 tsp	1 tsp
Turmeric	2.5 ml	¹/₂ tsp	¹/₂ tsp
Peanut butter	15 ml	1 tbsp	1 tbsp
Sunflower oil	15 ml	1 tbsp	1 tbsp
Soy sauce	15 ml	1 tbsp	1 tbsp
Salt and freshly ground black pepper			
Pork fillet, cubed	750 g	1¹/₂ lb	6 cups
Oil for fondue cooking			

METHOD

❶ Mix the coriander, turmeric, peanut butter, oil, soy sauce and salt and pepper together in a flat dish. Add the pork fillet and coat well. Cover and chill for 1 hour, stirring occasionally.

❷ Heat the oil in a fondue pot until bubbling. Serve.

Preparation time: 10 minutes plus marinating

Ale Batter Fondue

Perfect for dipping any meat or fish available. Try it this way with pork and chicken. Serve with Sweet Spicy Sauce (page 136), Herb Cream (page 127), Cranberry Relish (page 135) and Peppercorn Sauce (page 130).

SERVES 4

INGREDIENTS	METRIC	IMPERIAL	AMERICAN
Pork fillet, cubed	175 g	6 oz	1¹/₂ cups
Chicken breast fillets, cubed	2	2	2
Sunflower oil	45 ml	3 tbsp	3 tbsp
Garlic clove, crushed	1	1	1
Chopped oregano	5 ml	1 tsp	1 tsp
Sweet sherry	5 ml	1 tsp	1 tsp
Plain (all-purpose) flour	175 g	6 oz	1¹/₂ cups
Salt and freshly ground black pepper			
Eggs	2	2	2
Light ale	300 ml	¹/₂ pt	1¹/₄ cups
Oil for fondue cooking			

METHOD

❶ Place the pork and chicken in a bowl.

❷ Mix together the oil, garlic, oregano and sherry with some salt and freshly ground black pepper and pour over the meat. Chill for at least 1 hour.

❸ Sift the flour into a bowl, season with the salt and pepper and beat in the eggs. Blend in the light ale and whisk until smooth.

④ Dry the meat on kitchen paper and place in a serving bowl.

⑤ Heat the oil in a fondue pot until bubbling. Each person spears the meat on to the fondue fork then dips it into the batter and cooks it in the hot oil to suit their own taste.

Preparation time: 15 minutes

Minted Lamb Fondue

Serve these tiny meatballs with chunky chopped vegetables and any herb or garlic sauces (see sauce section, pages 120–139).

SERVES 4

INGREDIENTS	METRIC	IMPERIAL	AMERICAN
Minced (ground) lamb	450 g	1 lb	4 cups
Finely chopped mint	30 ml	2 tbsp	2 tbsp
Fresh breadcrumbs	75 g	3 oz	1¹/₂ cups
Salt and freshly ground black pepper			
Oil for fondue cooking			

METHOD

❶ Blend all the ingredients except the oil together and shape into 20 balls. Place on a serving plate and chill until required.

❷ Heat the oil in a fondue pot until bubbling and serve.

Preparation time: 10 minutes plus chilling

Too-Hot-To-Handle Steak

For those who like to add a little spice to their meal!

SERVES 4–6

INGREDIENTS	METRIC	IMPERIAL	AMERICAN
Oil	15 ml	1 tbsp	1 tbsp
Large onion, finely chopped	1	1	1
Garlic cloves, crushed	2	2	2
Can tomatoes	400 g	14 oz	1 large can
Tomato purée (paste)	30 ml	2 tbsp	2 tbsp
Green (bell) pepper, seeded and finely chopped	1	1	1
Chilli powder	2.5 ml	$1/2$ tsp	$1/2$ tsp
Worcestershire sauce	5 ml	1 tsp	1 tsp
Fresh green chilli, seeded and finely chopped	1	1	1
Salt and freshly ground black pepper			
Lean rump steak, cubed	750 g	$1^1/2$ lb	6 cups
Oil for fondue cooking			

METHOD

1 Heat the oil in a saucepan and add the onion and garlic. Cook until soft but not brown.

2 Stir in the tomatoes, tomato purée, green pepper, chilli powder and Worcestershire sauce. Simmer for 10 minutes. Remove from the heat and purée the sauce in a blender or processor.

❸ Put the sauce in a fondue pot, add the chopped chilli and season with the salt and pepper. Keep the sauce on a very low heat.

❹ Serve with a second fondue pot of hot oil heated until bubbling for cooking the meat.

Preparation time: 20 minutes

Meatball Fondue

Make the meatballs in advance and chill until ready to cook. Serve them with Cucumber and Mint Sauce (page 138) or Dill Cream (page 126), Cranberry Relish (page 135) and Red Pepper Sauce (page 134).

SERVES 4

INGREDIENTS	METRIC	IMPERIAL	AMERICAN
Minced (ground beef)	*350 g*	*12 oz*	*3 cups*
Minced (ground) pork	*350 g*	*12 oz*	*3 cups*
Onion, finely chopped	*1*	*1*	*1*
Slices of white bread,			
crumbed	*2*	*2*	*2*
Garlic cloves, crushed	*2*	*2*	*2*
English mustard	*20 ml*	*4 tsp*	*4 tsp*
Dried marjoram	*2.5 ml*	*¹/₂ tsp*	*¹/₂ tsp*
Dried thyme	*2.5 ml*	*¹/₂ tsp*	*¹/₂ tsp*
Chopped parsley	*30 ml*	*2 tbsp*	*2 tbsp*
Eggs	*2*	*2*	*2*
Milk	*120 ml*	*4 fl oz*	*¹/₂ cup*
Oil for fondue cooking			

METHOD

❶ Blend the meats well together.

❷ Add the remaining ingredients except the eggs and milk and mix well.

❸ Beat the eggs and milk together and use to bind the ingredients. Shape the mixture into small balls.

❹ Arrange on serving plates. Heat the oil in a fondue pot until bubbling and serve.

Preparation time: 10 minutes

Mixed Sausage Fondue

If you can't find cocktail-sized sausages, buy ordinary ones and cut them into 3 or 4 pieces. Serve with Mustard Sauce (page 131), Peppercorn Sauce (page 130) and Red Pepper Sauce (page 134).

SERVES 4

INGREDIENTS	METRIC	IMPERIAL	AMERICAN
Smoked pork ring, cut in 2.5 cm/1 in pieces	225 g	8 oz	$^1/_2$ lb
Cocktail-sized Frankfurters	225 g	8 oz	2 cups
Cocktail-sized Kabanos	225 g	8 oz	2 cups
Cocktail-sized pork and beef sausages	225 g	8 oz	2 cups
Oil for fondue cooking			

METHOD

❶ Arrange the sausages attractively on serving plates.

❷ Heat the oil until bubbling. Guests spear one sausage at a time and cook until sizzling. Serve with the dips, lots of crusty bread and a tomato salad.

Preparation time: 5 minutes

Crispy Duck with Pepper Sauce

The combination of the duck with the hot Red Pepper Sauce (page 134) makes a memorable fondue.

SERVES 4–6

INGREDIENTS	METRIC	IMPERIAL	AMERICAN
Butter	25 g	1 oz	2 tbsp
Onion, chopped	1	1	1
Red (bell) peppers, chopped	2	2	2
Garlic clove, crushed	1	1	1
Chicken stock	300 ml	¹/₂ pt	1¹/₄ cups
Plain (all-purpose) flour	30 ml	2 tbsp	2 tbsp
Salt and freshly ground black pepper			
Duck breast fillets, cut in bite-sized pieces	750 g	1¹/₂ lb	6 cups
Oil for fondue cooking			

METHOD

❶ Melt the butter and fry the chopped onion until soft but not brown. Stir in the red peppers and garlic.

❷ Cook gently for 5 minutes. Pour in the stock and season with some salt and freshly ground black pepper. Simmer for 15 minutes. Keep warm until ready to serve – or serve in a second fondue pot.

❸ Season the flour with the salt and pepper and coat the duck pieces. Arrange on serving plates.

4 Heat the oil in a fondue pot until bubbling. Fry the duck until crisp. Serve with the Red Pepper Sauce to dip into.

Preparation time: 25 minutes

Fondue Bourguignon

This classic mixed meat fondue can be altered to suit personal tastes.

SERVES 4–6

INGREDIENTS	METRIC	IMPERIAL	AMERICAN
Fillet steak, cubed	225 g	8 oz	2 cups
Lamb neck fillet, cubed	225 g	8 oz	2 cups
Pork fillet, cut in thin strips	225 g	8 oz	2 cups
Boneless chicken breasts,			
cut in thin strips	225 g	8 oz	2 cups
Lemon juice	45 ml	3 tbsp	3 tbsp
Salt and freshly ground			
black pepper			
Oil for fondue cooking			

METHOD

1 Sprinkle the meats with lemon juice, salt and pepper then arrange attractively on serving plates.

2 Heat the oil in a fondue pot until bubbling. Each guest spears a piece of meat, then cooks it to their own taste. Serve with a selection of sauces and dips (see page 120).

Preparation time: 15 minutes

Marinated Pork Fondue

Serve this succulent fondue with Cranberry Relish (page 135), Mustard Sauce (page 131) and Herb Cream (page 127).

SERVES 4

INGREDIENTS	METRIC	IMPERIAL	AMERICAN
Lean pork shoulder or fillet, cubed	*350 g*	*12 oz*	*3 cups*
Belly pork, rinded, boned and cubed	*350 g*	*12 oz*	*3 cups*
Frankfurters, cut in bite-sized pieces	*4*	*4*	*4*
Tomato ketchup (catsup)	*250 ml*	*8 fl oz*	*1 cup*
Wine vinegar	*120 ml*	*4 fl oz*	*¹/₂ cup*
Clear honey	*30 ml*	*2 tbsp*	*2 tbsp*
Garlic cloves, chopped	*2*	*2*	*2*
Dried marjoram	*2.5 ml*	*¹/₂ tsp*	*¹/₂ tsp*
Dried thyme	*2.5 ml*	*¹/₂ tsp*	*¹/₂ tsp*
Grated lemon rind	*10 ml*	*2 tsp*	*2 tsp*
Curry powder	*5 ml*	*1 tsp*	*1 tsp*
Pinch of cayenne			
Oil for fondue cooking			

METHOD

❶ Put the meats in a bowl. Mix the remaining ingredients, except the oil together and pour over. Mix then cover and chill for at least 5 hours, turning occasionally.

❷ Arrange on serving plates. Heat the oil in the fondue pot until bubbling then serve.

Preparation time: 10 minutes plus marinating

Beef Steak Fondue

Use rump, sirloin or fillet steak for this recipe. Serve with horseradish sauce, Mustard Sauce (page 131), Chinese Garlic Sauce (page 128) and Sweet Spicy Sauce (page 136).

SERVES 4

INGREDIENTS	METRIC	IMPERIAL	AMERICAN
Steak, cubed	750 g	1½ lb	6 cups
Olive oil	250 ml	8 fl oz	1 cup
Soy sauce	20 ml	4 tsp	4 tsp
Clear honey	10 ml	2 tsp	2 tsp
Garlic clove, chopped	1	1	1
Dried marjoram	5 ml	1 tsp	1 tsp
Dried thyme	5 ml	1 tsp	1 tsp
Pinch of cayenne			
Brandy	5 ml	1 tsp	1 tsp
Salt and freshly ground black pepper			
Oil for fondue cooking			

METHOD

❶ Put the meat in a bowl.

❷ Mix the remaining ingredients together and pour over the meat. Toss well then cover and chill for at least 5 hours, turning occasionally.

❸ Arrange the meat on serving plates. Heat the oil in a fondue pot until bubbling and serve.

Preparation time: 10 minutes plus marinating

Birds of a Feather Fondue

Serve with Whipped Pineapple Sauce (page 121), Herb Cream (page 127), Chinese Garlic Sauce (page 128), and Ginger Sauce (page 137).

SERVES 4

INGREDIENTS	METRIC	IMPERIAL	AMERICAN
Broccoli florets	100 g	4 oz	1 cup
Carrots, sliced	100 g	4 oz	1 cup
Celery, cut in chunks	100 g	4 oz	1 cup
Button mushrooms	100 g	4 oz	1 cup
Lemon juice	2.5 ml	¹/₂ tsp	¹/₂ tsp
Worcestershire sauce	2.5 ml	¹/₂ tsp	¹/₂ tsp
Chicken breast fillets, cut in bite-sized pieces	2	2	2
Duck breast fillets, cut in bite-sized pieces	2	2	2
Pheasant breasts, cut in bite-sized pieces	2	2	2
Salt and freshly ground black pepper			
Cornflour (cornstarch)	30 ml	2 tbsp	2 tbsp
Oil for fondue cooking			

METHOD

❶ Cook the broccoli, carrots and celery in boiling water for 3 minutes until almost tender. Drain, rinse with cold water and pat dry on kitchen paper.

❷ Sprinkle the mushrooms with the lemon juice and Worcestershire sauce.

❸ Arrange the meat and mushrooms on serving plates. Toss the vegetables in a little salt and pepper and the cornflour and arrange alongside.

❹ Heat the oil in a fondue pot until bubbling and serve.

Preparation time: 15 minutes

Greek Fondue

Serve with pitta bread, a dish of chopped nuts and Cucumber and Mint Sauce (page 138), Herb Cream (page 127) and Cranberry Relish (page 135).

SERVES 4–6

INGREDIENTS	METRIC	IMPERIAL	AMERICAN
Minced (ground) lamb	350 g	12 oz	3 cups
Onion, chopped	1	1	1
Fresh breadcrumbs	30 ml	2 tbsp	2 tbsp
Garlic clove, crushed	1	1	1
Paprika	5 ml	1 tsp	1 tsp
Salt and freshly ground black pepper			
Dried mint	5 ml	1 tsp	1 tsp
Egg, beaten	1	1	1
Lamb fillet, cubed	175 g	6 oz	1¹/₂ cups
Chicken breast, cubed	175 g	6 oz	1¹/₂ cups
Red (bell) pepper, cut in chunks	1	1	1
Green (bell) pepper, cut in chunks	1	1	1
Small aubergine (eggplant) cut in chunks	1	1	1
Small courgettes (zucchini) cut in chunks	2	2	2
Oil for fondue cooking			

METHOD

❶ Mix the minced lamb with the onion, breadcrumbs, garlic, paprika, a little salt and pepper and the mint. Bind with beaten egg.

2 Shape into small balls and arrange on serving plates with the cubed meats and the vegetables.

3 Heat the oil in a fondue pot until bubbling and serve.

Preparation time: 15 minutes

Fiery Lamb Fondue

This is a fondue with attitude! If you don't like your food too hot, add less cayenne to the marinade.

Serve with pitta bread and Garlic Sauce (page 133), Herb Cream (page 127) and Cucumber and Mint Sauce (page 138).

SERVES 4

INGREDIENTS	METRIC	IMPERIAL	AMERICAN
Lamb fillet, cubed	750 g	1¹/₂ lb	6 cups
Olive oil	150 ml	¹/₄ pt	²/₃ cup
Salt	5 ml	1 tsp	1 tsp
Garlic cloves, chopped	2	2	2
Grated lemon rind	10 ml	2 tsp	2 tsp
Cayenne	5 ml	1 tsp	1 tsp
Dried thyme	2.5 ml	¹/₂ tsp	¹/₂ tsp
Dried rosemary	2.5 ml	¹/₂ tsp	¹/₂ tsp
Dried mint	2.5 ml	¹/₂ tsp	¹/₂ tsp
Black pepper	5 ml	1 tsp	1 tsp
Oil for fondue cooking			

METHOD

❶ Put the meat in a bowl.

❷ Mix the remaining ingredients together, except the oil, and pour over the meat. Mix well. Cover and chill for at least 4 hours, turning occasionally.

❸ Arrange meat on serving plates. Heat the oil in a fondue pot until bubbling and serve.

Preparation time: 10 minutes plus marinating

Rustic Fondue

Make sure that you buy thin lamb cutlets or they'll take too long to cook. Serve with Herb Cream (page 127), Mustard Sauce (page 131), horseradish sauce and Cheese and Onion Sauce (page 139).

SERVES 4

INGREDIENTS	METRIC	IMPERIAL	AMERICAN
Thin lamb cutlets	8-12	8-12	8-12
Garlic clove, chopped	1	1	1
Dried thyme	5 ml	1 tsp	1 tsp
Dried marjoram	2.5 ml	$^1/_2$ tsp	$^1/_2$ tsp
Olive oil	45 ml	3 tbsp	3 tbsp
Salt and freshly ground black pepper			
Thick, herby pork sausages, cut in chunks	4	4	4
Cherry tomatoes	8-12	8-12	8-12
Red (bell) pepper, diced	1	1	1
Green (bell) pepper, diced	1	1	1
Oil for fondue cooking			

METHOD

❶ Lay the cutlets in a large shallow dish.

❷ Mix the garlic, herbs and olive oil with a little salt and pepper and pour over, coating completely. Cover and leave for at least 30 minutes. Arrange on serving plates with the sausages, tomatoes and peppers.

❸ Heat the oil in a fondue pot until bubbling and serve.

Preparation time: 10 minutes plus chilling

Pork and Vegetable Fondue

Vegetarians can have all tofu and no pork. Those who dislike tofu can have more pork! Serve with Herb Cream (page 127), Mustard Sauce (page 131), Cucumber and Mint Sauce (page 138) and Sweet Spicy Sauce (page 136).

SERVES 4

INGREDIENTS	METRIC	IMPERIAL	AMERICAN
Cauliflower florets	150 g	5 oz	1¼ cups
Broccoli florets	150 g	5 oz	1¼ cups
Carrots, sliced	150 g	5 oz	1¼ cups
Bunch of spring onions (scallions), cut in 2.5 cm/1 in pieces			
Cornflour (cornstarch)	45 ml	3 tbsp	3 tbsp
Salt and freshly ground black pepper			
Pork fillet, cubed	450 g	1 lb	4 cups
Tofu, cubed	175 g	6 oz	1½ cups
Oil for fondue cooking			

METHOD

❶ Cook the vegetables in boiling water for 3 minutes until just tender. Drain, rinse with cold water and dry on kitchen paper. Toss in the cornflour seasoned with a little salt and pepper.

❷ Arrange the vegetables with the pork and tofu on serving plates.

❸ Heat the oil in a fondue pot until bubbling and serve.

Preparation time: 15 minutes

Country Fondue

Serve with Dill Cream (page 126), Mustard Sauce (page 131), Cranberry Relish (page 135) and Fines Herbes Sauce (page 129).

SERVES 4

INGREDIENTS	METRIC	IMPERIAL	AMERICAN
Chicken breast fillets,			
cubed	*2*	*2*	*2*
Turkey breast fillets,			
cubed	*2*	*2*	*2*
Juice of 1 lemon			
Worcestershire sauce	*5 ml*	*1 tsp*	*1 tsp*
Salt and freshly ground			
black pepper			
Cornflour (cornstarch)	*30 ml*	*2 tbsp*	*2 tbsp*
Button (pearl) onions	*12*	*12*	*12*
Carrots, cut in small chunks	*4*	*4*	*4*
Oil for fondue cooking			

METHOD

1 Put the poultry in a bowl and sprinkle with the lemon juice, Worcestershire sauce and a little salt and pepper. Toss well. Chill for at least 10 minutes.

2 Dust with cornflour then arrange on serving plates.

3 Meanwhile, cook the onions and carrots in boiling water for 3 minutes. Drain. Rinse with cold water and dry on kitchen paper. Arrange on plates with the poultry.

4 Heat the oil in a fondue pot until bubbling and serve.

Preparation time: 15 minutes plus chilling

Gourmet Fondue

Serve this delicious combination of meat and vegetables with Cocktail Sauce (page 124), Caviar Sauce (page 125), Cheese and Onion Sauce (page 139) and Peppercorn Sauce (page 130).

SERVES 4

INGREDIENTS	METRIC	IMPERIAL	AMERICAN
Broccoli florets	*100 g*	*4 oz*	*1 cup*
Carrots, cut in strips	*100 g*	*4 oz*	*1 cup*
French beans, trimmed and			
cut in halves	*225 g*	*8 oz*	*2 cups*
Streaky bacon rashers			
(slices)	*8-12*	*8-12*	*8-12*
Fillet steak, cut in strips	*175 g*	*6 oz*	*1¹/₂ cups*
Lamb fillet, cut in strips	*175 g*	*6 oz*	*1¹/₂ cups*
Pork fillet, cut in strips	*175 g*	*6 oz*	*1¹/₂ cups*
Oil for fondue cooking			

METHOD

❶ Cook the vegetables for 3 minutes in boiling water. Drain, rinse with cold water and dry on kitchen paper.

❷ Divide the beans in 8 or 12 bundles and wrap a piece of bacon firmly round each.

❸ Arrange on individual serving plates with the other vegetables and the meats.

❹ Heat the oil in a fondue pot until bubbling and serve.

Preparation time: 10 minutes

Trieste Fondue

Serve this fondue with a dish of chopped toasted almonds as well as the following dips: Cocktail Sauce (page 124), Herb Cream (page 127) and Mustard Sauce (page 131).

SERVES 4

INGREDIENTS	METRIC	IMPERIAL	AMERICAN
Pork fillet, cut in strips	750 g	1¹/₂ lb	6 cups
Garlic cloves, crushed	2	2	2
Salt	5 ml	1 tsp	1 tsp
Grated lemon rind	5 ml	1 tsp	1 tsp
Dried basil	5 ml	1 tsp	1 tsp
Dried thyme	5 ml	1 tsp	1 tsp
Olive oil	250 ml	8 fl oz	1 cup
Lemon juice	2.5 ml	¹/₂ tsp	¹/₂ tsp
Worcestershire sauce	2.5 ml	¹/₂ tsp	¹/₂ tsp
Oil for fondue cooking			

METHOD

❶ Put the pork in a bowl. Mix together the garlic, salt, lemon rind, herbs and olive oil to make a marinade.

❷ Sprinkle the meat with the lemon juice and the Worcestershire sauce then pour the marinade over.

❸ Toss well, cover and chill for at least 1 hour, turning occasionally.

❹ Arrange the meat on a serving dish. Heat the oil in a fondue pot until bubbling and serve.

Preparation time: 15 minutes plus marinating

SIMMERING STOCK FONDUES

When you transfer the stock to the table, keep it gently bubbling so the temperature remains consistent for cooking.

Oriental Beef Fondue

Use any sauces and dips you like with the meat, but if you want to keep the Far Eastern flavour, offer a bowl of soy sauce as one of the accompaniments and serve thin strips of raw vegetables to dip too.

SERVES 4–6

INGREDIENTS	METRIC	IMPERIAL	AMERICAN
Fillet, sirloin or rump steak,			
cut in thin strips	*750 g*	*1¹/₂ lb*	*6 cups*
Small sprigs of parsley	*4-6*	*4-6*	*4-6*
Grated fresh root ginger	*5 ml*	*1 tsp*	*1 tsp*
Beef stock	*1.5 L*	*2¹/₂ pts*	*6 cups*
Sweet sherry	*150 ml*	*¹/₄ pt*	*²/₃ cup*

METHOD

❶ Arrange the meat on individual serving plates. Garnish with sprigs of parsley.

❷ Put the ginger and stock in a fondue pot and heat until bubbling. Guests spear a piece of meat and cook in the stock to required doneness.

❸ When all the meat has been cooked and eaten, add the sherry to the stock in the pot. Heat through then ladle into soup cups and hand round.

Preparation time: 10 minutes

Fondue Hotpot

Almost any cooked vegetables can be added to this meal. Each person uses Chinese wire strainers to dip the food in the stock before eating.

SERVES 4–6

INGREDIENTS	METRIC	IMPERIAL	AMERICAN
Chicken stock	1.75 L	3 pts	7^1/$_2$ cups
Garlic clove, crushed	1	1	1
Chopped tarragon	2.5 ml	^{1}/$_2$ tsp	^{1}/$_2$ tsp
Onion, finely chopped	1	1	1
Dry sherry	30 ml	2 tbsp	2 tbsp
Lamb fillet	750 g	1^1/$_2$ lb	1^1/$_2$ lb
Green (bell) pepper, seeded and chopped	1	1	1
Red (bell) pepper, seeded and chopped	1	1	1
New potatoes, boiled	450 g	1 lb	1 lb

METHOD

❶ Put the stock in a saucepan and bring to the boil.

❷ Add the garlic, tarragon and chopped onion and simmer for 30 minutes until the stock has reduced.

❸ Stir in the sherry and continue cooking for 5 minutes. Transfer to a fondue pot and keep the heat low.

❹ Slice the lamb very thinly and arrange on a large plate with the red and green pepper and the boiled potatoes. Serve.

Preparation time: 35 minutes

Chinese Noodle Fondue

A whole Chinese meal in the pot! Serve the meat with small bowls of fried rice, soy sauce and Sweet and Sour Sauce (page 122). Then add the noodles to the pot for an authentic oriental-flavoured soup. A beansprout and cucumber salad makes a refreshing accompaniment too.

SERVES 4

INGREDIENTS	METRIC	IMPERIAL	AMERICAN
Boneless turkey or chicken			
breasts	*4*	*4*	*4*
Soy sauce	*30 ml*	*2 tbsp*	*2 tbsp*
Ground ginger	*2.5 ml*	*¹/₂ tsp*	*¹/₂ tsp*
Quick-cook Chinese noodles	*100 g*	*4 oz*	*1 cup*
Chicken stock (made with			
3 stock cubes)	*1.5 L*	*2¹/₂ pts*	*6 cups*
Prawn crackers			

METHOD

❶ Cut the turkey or chicken into thin strips diagonally.

❷ Sprinkle with soy sauce and ginger, toss well and leave to marinate in the fridge for 1–2 hours.

❸ Put the noodles in a bowl, cover with boiling water, leave to stand for 5 minutes then drain and place in a bowl.

❹ Heat the stock in a fondue pot until bubbling. Guests spear a piece of meat then cook in the stock. When all the meat has been cooked, add the noodles to the pot. Ladle into soup bowls and serve with prawn crackers.

Preparation time: 15 minutes plus marinating

Welsh Lamb Fondue

For convenience use canned drained carrots and potatoes, but the flavour isn't as good. Serve redcurrant jelly and Cheese and Onion Sauce (page 139) with the meat and vegetables then lots of warm soda bread with the leek soup.

SERVES 4

INGREDIENTS	METRIC	IMPERIAL	AMERICAN
Boned leg, shoulder or neck fillet of lamb, cut in thin strips	*450 g*	*1 lb*	*4 cups*
Baby carrots, scraped	*225 g*	*8 oz*	*2 cups*
Baby potatoes, scrubbed	*450 g*	*1 lb*	*4 cups*
Leeks, sliced	*4*	*4*	*4*
Chicken or lamb stock (made with 3 stock cubes)	*1.5 L*	*2¹/₂ pts*	*6 cups*
Freshly ground black pepper			

METHOD

❶ Arrange the meat on a serving plate.

❷ Parboil the carrots and potatoes for 5 minutes until almost tender. Drain, rinse with cold water and drain again. Put with the meat.

❸ Simmer the leeks in the stock in a fondue pot for 5 minutes until almost tender.

❹ Keep the stock simmering and cook pieces of meat, potato and carrot to taste. Season the leek stock in the pot with pepper and ladle into soup bowls.

Preparation time: 10 minutes

Sweet and Sour Fondue

Serve this savoury combination with a dish of mixed pickles, and with Garlic Sauce (page 133), Ginger Sauce (page 137) and Mustard Sauce (page 131).

SERVES 4-6

INGREDIENTS	METRIC	IMPERIAL	AMERICAN
Pork sausagemeat	225 g	8 oz	2 cups
Fresh breadcrumbs	30 ml	2 tbsp	2 tbsp
Dried mixed herbs	5 ml	1 tsp	1 tsp
Egg, beaten	1	1	1
Glass dry white wine	1	1	1
Lamb, pork or beef stock	750 ml	1¼ pts	3 cups
White wine vinegar	5 ml	1 tsp	1 tsp
Onions, sliced	3	3	3
Bay leaves	2	2	2
Cloves	3	3	3
Mustard seeds	2.5 ml	½ tsp	½ tsp
Peppercorns	6	6	6
Light brown sugar	15 ml	1 tbsp	1 tbsp
Salt and freshly ground black pepper			
Pork fillet, cut in strips	175 g	6 oz	1½ cups
Lamb fillet, cut in strips	175 g	6 oz	1½ cups
Kabanos, sliced thickly	225 g	8 oz	2 cups

METHOD

❶ Work the sausagemeat, breadcrumbs and herbs together then mix with the beaten egg and shape into small balls. Chill until ready to serve.

❷ Bring the wine, stock and vinegar to the boil in a fondue pot or saucepan on top of the stove. Add the onions and the remaining flavourings and simmer for 8–10 minutes.

❸ Pour into a fondue pot, if necessary, and transfer to the table. Arrange the meats and sausage balls on serving plates and serve.

Preparation time: 20 minutes

Supper Sausage Fondue

Serve this tasty combination with Herb Cream (page 127), horseradish sauce and Mustard Sauce (page 131).

SERVES 4

INGREDIENTS	METRIC	IMPERIAL	AMERICAN
Pork sausagemeat	225 g	8 oz	2 cups
Fresh breadcrumbs	30 ml	2 tbsp	2 tbsp
Egg, beaten	1	1	1
Chicken stock	750 ml	1¼ pts	3 cups
Light ale	150 ml	¼ pt	⅔ cup
Vinegar	5 ml	1 tsp	1 tsp
Golden (light corn) syrup	15 ml	1 tbsp	1 tbsp
Dried marjoram	5 ml	1 tsp	1 tsp
Onions, cut in chunks	2	2	2
Carrots, sliced	2	2	2
Red (bell) pepper, cut in chunks	1	1	1
Green (bell) pepper, cut in chunks	1	1	1
Small salami sausage, cut in slices and skinned	1	1	1
Frankfurters, cut in chunks	4	4	4
Turkey sausages, cut in chunks	4	4	4

METHOD

❶ Mix the sausagemeat with the breadcrumbs and egg and shape into small balls. Chill until ready to serve.

2 Put the stock, ale, vinegar, syrup and marjoram in a fondue pot or saucepan and simmer for 8 minutes on the stove. Transfer to a fondue pot, if necessary, and place on the table.

3 Arrange the vegetables, sausages and sausage balls on serving plates and serve.

Preparation time: 10 minutes plus chilling

Gammon Plus Fondue

Serve with a dish of mixed pickles, Whipped Pineapple Sauce (page 121), and Mustard Sauce (page 131).

SERVES 4–6

INGREDIENTS	METRIC	IMPERIAL	AMERICAN
Glass dry white wine	*1*	*1*	*1*
Pork stock	*500 ml*	*17 fl oz*	*2¹/₄ cups*
Onion, studded with 3 cloves	*1*	*1*	*1*
Freshly ground black pepper			
Crème frâiche	*150 ml*	*¹/₄ pt*	*²/₃ cup*
Baby leeks, cut in pieces	*4*	*4*	*4*
Button mushrooms	*225 g*	*8 oz*	*2 cups*
Raw lean gammon, cubed	*175 g*	*6 oz*	*1¹/₂ cups*
Boiled ham in one piece, cubed	*175 g*	*6 oz*	*1¹/₂ cups*
Smoked pork loin, cubed	*100 g*	*4 oz*	*1 cup*
Pork fillet, cubed	*175 g*	*6 oz*	*1¹/₂ cups*

METHOD

❶ Put the wine, stock, onion and pepper in a fondue pot or saucepan and simmer for 8 minutes on the stove. Transfer to a fondue pot, if necessary, and place on the table. Stir in the crème frâiche.

❷ Arrange the vegetables and meat on serving plates and serve.

Preparation time: 15 minutes

Fondue for Kings

Serve with Whipped Pineapple Sauce (page 121), Herb Cream (page 127) and Cranberry Relish (page 135).

SERVES 6

INGREDIENTS	METRIC	IMPERIAL	AMERICAN
Carrots, sliced	4	4	4
Broccoli florets	225 g	8 oz	2 cups
Dry white wine	500 ml	17 fl oz	2^1/$_4$ cups
Beef stock	500 ml	17 fl oz	2^1/$_4$ cups
Bay leaves	2	2	2
Cloves	3	3	3
Peppercorns	6	6	6
Sprigs of thyme or tarragon	2	2	2
Salt and freshly ground black pepper			
Veal fillet, cubed	175 g	6 oz	1^1/$_2$ cups
Turkey breast fillet, cut in strips	75 g	6 oz	1^1/$_2$ cups
Goose or duck breast fillet, cut in strips	175 g	6 oz	1^1/$_2$ cups
Venison fillet, cubed	175 g	6 oz	1^1/$_2$ cups

METHOD

❶ Cook the vegetables in boiling water for 2 minutes. Drain, rinse with cold water and dry on kitchen paper.

❷ Simmer the wine, stock and flavourings for 8 minutes. Place on the table.

❸ Arrange the food on serving plates and serve.

Preparation time: 15 minutes

Herb Fondue

Serve this fragrant fondue with Cheese and Onion Sauce (page 139), horseradish sauce, Cucumber and Mint Sauce (page 138) and Garlic Sauce (page 133).

SERVES 4

INGREDIENTS	METRIC	IMPERIAL	AMERICAN
Cauliflower florets	225 g	8 oz	2 cups
Broccoli florets	225 g	8 oz	2 cups
Asparagus, cut in short lengths	175 g	6 oz	1¹/₂ cups
Chicken stock	750 ml	1¹/₄ pts	3 cups
Dry white wine	250 ml	8 fl oz	1 cup
Onions, studded with 2 cloves each	2	2	2
Sprig each of tarragon, basil and oregano			
Garlic cloves, chopped	2	2	2
Chicken breast fillet, cut in strips	225 g	8 oz	2 cups
Rabbit fillet, cut in strips	225 g	8 oz	2 cups

METHOD

❶ Cook the vegetables for 2 minutes in boiling water. Drain, rinse with cold water and dry on kitchen paper.

❷ Put the stock, wine, onions, herbs and garlic in a fondue pot or a saucepan on top of the stove, bring to the boil and simmer for 8 minutes. Remove the herbs, transfer to a fondue pot, if necessary, and place on the table.

❸ Arrange the meat and vegetables on serving plates, serve.

Preparation time: 15 minutes

Sparkling French Fondue

Serve with Whipped Pineapple Sauce (page 121), Fines Herbes Sauce (page 129) and Red Pepper Sauce (page 134).

SERVES 4

INGREDIENTS	METRIC	IMPERIAL	AMERICAN
Broccoli florets	100 g	4 oz	1 cup
Carrots, sliced	100 g	4 oz	1 cup
Baby corn cobs	100 g	4 oz	1 cup
Bunch of spring onions (scallions)			
Beef stock	500 ml	17 fl oz	2¹/₄ cups
Sparkling white wine	250 ml	8 fl oz	1 cup
Double (heavy) cream	150 ml	¹/₄ pt	²/₃ cup
Sprigs of tarragon	2	2	2
Pinch of saffron strands			
Salt and freshly ground black pepper			
Stuffed vine leaves	8	8	8
Fillet steak, cubed	175 g	6 oz	1¹/₂ cups
Venison fillet, cubed	100 g	4 oz	1 cup
Lamb fillet, cubed	175 g	6 oz	1¹/₂ cups

METHOD

❶ Cook the vegetables in boiling water for 2 minutes. Drain, rinse with cold water and dry on kitchen paper.

❷ Simmer the stock, wine, cream, tarragon and saffron for 5 minutes. Remove the herbs and season. Pour into a fondue pot, if necessary, and place on the table.

❸ Arrange the food on serving plates and serve.

Preparation time: 15 minutes

Forester's Fondue

Serve with Mustard Sauce (page 131), Dill Cream (page 126), Cranberry Relish (page 135) and Fines Herbes Sauce (page 129).

SERVES 4

INGREDIENTS	METRIC	IMPERIAL	AMERICAN
Glass red wine	*1*	*1*	*1*
Beef stock	*500 ml*	*17 fl oz*	*2¹/₄ cups*
Double (heavy) cream	*150 ml*	*¹/₄ pt*	*²/₃ cup*
Cranberry sauce	*30 ml*	*2 tbsp*	*2 tbsp*
Sprig of marjoram			
Sprig of thyme			
Salt and freshly ground black pepper			
Blue cheese, crumbled	*15 ml*	*1 tbsp*	*1 tbsp*
Venison fillet, cubed	*175 g*	*6 oz*	*1¹/₂ cups*
Pork fillet, cubed	*350 g*	*12 oz*	*3 cups*
Raw lean gammon, cubed	*100 g*	*4 oz*	*1 cup*
Button mushrooms	*100 g*	*4 oz*	*1 cup*
Bunch of spring onions (scallions) cut into 5 cm/2 in lengths			

METHOD

❶ Put the wine, stock, cream, cranberry sauce and herbs in a fondue pot or a saucepan and simmer for 5 minutes. Remove the herbs and season with salt and pepper. Transfer to a fondue pot, if necessary, and place on the table. Stir in the cheese until melted.

❷ Arrange the meats and vegetables on serving plates, serve.

Preparation time: 15 minutes

Blushing Mixed Fondue

This flavoursome fondue is best served with horseradish sauce, tartare sauce, Chinese Garlic Sauce (page 128) and Red Pepper Sauce (page 134).

SERVES 4

INGREDIENTS	METRIC	IMPERIAL	AMERICAN
Mixed vegetable juice	300 ml	$^1/_2$ pt	$1^1/_4$ cups
Glass red wine	1	1	1
Beef stock	600 ml	1 pt	$2^1/_2$ cups
Garlic cloves, chopped	2	2	2
Sprig of thyme			
Sprig of marjoram			
Salt and freshly ground black pepper			
Pork fillet, cubed	175 g	6 oz	$1^1/_2$ cups
Rump steak, cubed	175 g	6 oz	$1^1/_2$ cups
Turkey breast fillet, cut in strips	175 g	6 oz	$1^1/_2$ cups
Frankfurters, cut in chunks	4	4	4
Red (bell) pepper, cut in chunks	1	1	1
Cherry tomatoes	8-12	8-12	8-12
Baby beetroot (red beets)	8-12	8-12	8-12

METHOD

❶ Simmer the vegetable juice, wine, stock and seasonings for 8 minutes. Remove the herbs. Transfer to a fondue pot on the table, if necessary.

❷ Arrange the meat and vegetables on serving plates and serve.

Preparation time: 15 minutes

Fonduta Di Napoli

For a less expensive fondue, omit the steak and double the quantity of ravioli. Serve with Garlic Sauce (page 133), Cocktail Sauce (page 124) and Red Pepper Sauce (page 134) plus lots of ciabatta bread to mop up the fondue when all the meat, pasta and vegetables have been eaten.

SERVES 4

INGREDIENTS	METRIC	IMPERIAL	AMERICAN
Broccoli florets	100 g	4 oz	1 cup
Mangetout (snow peas)	100 g	4 oz	1 cup
Cherry tomatoes	8-12	8-12	8-12
Butter	25 g	1 oz	2 tbsp
Garlic clove, crushed	1	1	1
Onion, chopped	1	1	1
Can chopped tomatoes	400 g	14 oz	1 large can
Beef stock	250 ml	8 fl oz	1 cup
Sprig of oregano			
Sprig of basil			
Grated Parmesan cheese	30 ml	2 tbsp	2 tbsp
Grated lemon rind	5 ml	1 tsp	1 tsp
Salt and freshly ground black pepper			
Fillet steak, cubed	225 g	8 oz	2 cups
Raw, lean gammon, cubed	225 g	8 oz	2 cups
Fresh or dried ravioli, cooked	225 g	8 oz	2 cups

METHOD

❶ Cook the broccoli and mangetout for 2 minutes in boiling water. Drain, rinse with cold water and dry on kitchen paper.

❷ Heat the butter in a fondue pot on top of the stove. Add the garlic and onion and fry (sauté) until pale golden brown, stirring. Add the chopped tomatoes, stock and herbs and simmer for 8 minutes. Remove the herbs.

❸ Stir in the Parmesan and lemon and season to taste.

❹ Transfer to the table. Arrange the meat, pasta and vegetables on serving plates and serve:

Note: The pasta is already cooked so will only need to be kept in the pot long enough to heat through.

Preparation time: 15 minutes

Cheesy Cream Fondue

Serve this with Fines Herbes Sauce (page 129), Peppercorn Sauce (page 130) and Hot Curry Sauce (page 132).

SERVES 4

INGREDIENTS	METRIC	IMPERIAL	AMERICAN
Celery, cut into chunks	175 g	6 oz	1¹/₂ cups
Glass dry white wine	1	1	1
Chicken stock	750 ml	1¹/₄ pts	3 cups
Double (heavy) cream	150 ml	¹/₄ pt	²/₃ cup
Grated Parmesan cheese	30 ml	2 tbsp	2 tbsp
Sprig of oregano			
Sprig of basil			
Salt and freshly ground black pepper			
Cherry tomatoes	12	12	12
Chicken breast fillet, cut in thin strips	175 g	6 oz	1¹/₂ cups
Pork fillet, cut in thin strips	175 g	6 oz	1¹/₂ cups
Calves' or lambs' liver, cut in thin strips	175 g	6 oz	1¹/₂ cups

METHOD

❶ Cook the celery in boiling water for 3 minutes. Drain, rinse with cold water and dry on kitchen paper. Reserve.

❷ Bring the wine, stock and cream to the boil. Stir in the cheese and herbs and leave for 5 minutes. Remove the herbs and season to taste.

❸ Arrange the celery, tomatoes and meat on serving plates. Heat the stock until gently simmering then serve.

Preparation time: 15 minutes

Garden Fondue

Serve with Garlic Sauce (page 133), Fines Herbes Sauce (page 129) and Cocktail Sauce (page 124). For vegetarians, serve tofu instead of steak.

SERVES 4

INGREDIENTS	METRIC	IMPERIAL	AMERICAN
Broccoli florets	175 g	6 oz	1¹/₂ cups
Cauliflower florets	175 g	6 oz	1¹/₂ cups
Carrots, sliced	4	4	4
Celery stick, cut in chunks	1	1	1
Onions, cut in wedges	4	4	4
Glass dry white wine	1	1	1
Vegetable stock	500 ml	17 fl oz	2¹/₄ cups
Dried oregano	5 ml	1 tsp	1 tsp
Whipping cream	150 ml	¹/₄ pt	²/₃ cup
Cornflour (cornstarch)	15 ml	1 tbsp	1 tbsp
Lemon juice	2.5 ml	¹/₂ tsp	¹/₂ tsp
Salt and freshly ground black pepper			
Fillet steak, cut in strips	450 g	1 lb	4 cups

METHOD

❶ Cook the vegetables in boiling water for 3 minutes. Drain, rinse with cold water and dry on kitchen paper.

❷ Bring the wine, stock and herbs to the boil. Blend the cream and cornflour together, stir into the pot and cook, stirring, until thick. Add the lemon juice and season.

❸ Arrange the vegetables and meat on plates and serve.

Preparation time: 20 minutes

Witch's Fondue

Substitute crab sticks, cut in chunks, for lobster tails if you prefer. Offer a good range of dips, such as Dill Cream (page 126), Mustard Sauce (page 131), Caviar Sauce (page 125) and Cocktail Sauce (page 124) plus a good-sized dish of mixed pickles.

SERVES 4–6

INGREDIENTS	METRIC	IMPERIAL	AMERICAN
Lobster tails	175 g	6 oz	1¹/₂ cups
Juice of ¹/₂ lemon			
Brandy	5 ml	1 tsp	1 tsp
Worcestershire sauce	2.5 ml	¹/₂ tsp	¹/₂ tsp
Small leeks, cut in pieces	2	2	2
Carrots, sliced	2	2	2
Celery sticks, cut in chunks	2	2	2
Glass dry white wine	1	1	1
Beef stock	750 ml	1¹/₄ pts	3 cups
Medium sherry	60 ml	4 tbsp	4 tbsp
Onion, studded with			
3 cloves	1	1	1
Chopped dill (dillweed)	15 ml	1 tbsp	1 tbsp
Fillet steak, cubed	175 g	6 oz	1¹/₂ cups
Veal fillet, cubed	175 g	6 oz	1¹/₂ cups
Pork fillet, cubed	175 g	6 oz	1¹/₂ cups

METHOD

❶ Put the lobster tails in a bowl. Sprinkle with lemon juice, brandy and Worcestershire sauce.

❷ Cook the vegetables in boiling water for 3 minutes. Drain, rinse with cold water and dry on kitchen paper.

❸ Put the wine, stock and sherry in a fondue pot. Add the onion and dill. Bring to the boil then leave to stand for 5 minutes. Remove the onion.

❹ Arrange the lobster, vegetables and meat on serving plates and serve.

Preparation time: 20 minutes

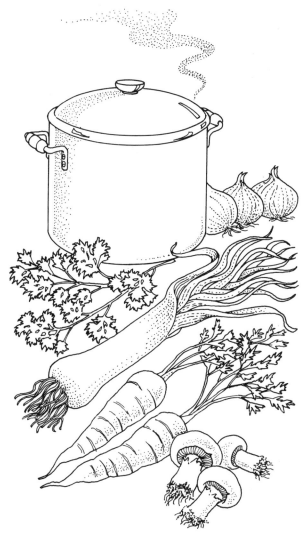

Speciality Fondues

Try a Greek Metze Fondue, an Indian Extravaganza, a Chinese Complete Creation or other international delights.

Metze Fondue

Serve Cucumber and Mint Sauce (page 138), dishes of mixed pickles, taramasalata and hummous (from a delicatessen counter), a Greek salad made with lettuce, cucumber, tomato, onion, feta cheese and olives dressed with olive oil, vinegar and black pepper plus lots of warm pitta or sesame and caraway seed bread.

SERVES 6–8

INGREDIENTS	METRIC	IMPERIAL	AMERICAN
Greek Fondue (page 62)			
Haloumi cheese	*225 g*	*8 oz*	*¹/₂ lb*
Streaky bacon rashers			
(slices)	*6-8*	*6-8*	*6-8*
Squid in batter	*225 g*	*8 oz*	*2 cups*
Stuffed vine leaves	*6-8*	*6-8*	*6-8*
Oil for fondue cooking			

METHOD

❶ Prepare the Greek Fondue as in the recipe. Arrange on serving plates.

❷ Cut the cheese into 6 or 8 slices. Wrap a piece of bacon around each and secure with wooden skewers. Arrange on a separate plate. Arrange squid and vine leaves on other plates.

❸ Heat the oil in a fondue pot until bubbling. Guests start with the squid and then the cheese, then the vine leaves and finish with the meat and vegetables.

Preparation time: 20 minutes

Chinese Complete Creation

Serve with Chinese Garlic Sauce (page 128), Ginger Sauce (page 137), soy sauce, a bowl of quick-cooked noodles and a salad of fresh beansprouts, red and green (bell) peppers, spring onion (scallion) and grated carrot, dressed with oil, wine vinegar and a dash of soy sauce.

SERVES 6

INGREDIENTS	METRIC	IMPERIAL	AMERICAN
Farmer's Fondue (page 48)			
For the sweet and sour sauce			
Pineapple juice	300 ml	¹/₂ pt	1¹/₄ cups
Vinegar	15 ml	1 tbsp	1 tbsp
Tomato ketchup (catsup)	30 ml	2 tbsp	2 tbsp
Cornflour (cornstarch)	15 ml	1 tbsp	1 tbsp
Soy sauce	15 ml	1 tbsp	1 tbsp
For the batter			
Plain (all-purpose) flour	100 g	4 oz	1 cup
Pinch of salt			
Water	300 ml	¹/₂ pt	1¹/₄ cups
Egg white	1	1	1
Can water chestnuts	250 g	9 oz	1 small can
Cornflour (cornstarch) for dusting			
Belly pork, cubed	225 g	8 oz	2 cups
Ready-to-cook spring rolls	6	6	6
Chinese chicken wings (uncooked)	6-12	6-12	6-12
Button mushrooms	12	12	12
Baby corn cobs	12	12	12
Oil for fondue cooking			

METHOD

❶ Prepare the Farmer's Fondue.

❷ Make the sauce. Whisk all the ingredients together in a saucepan. Bring to the boil and cook for 2 minutes, stirring, until thickened. Pour into a small dish when ready to serve.

❸ Make the batter. Put the flour and salt in a bowl. Whisk in the water. Whisk the egg white until stiff and fold in with a metal spoon. Put in individual bowls.

❹ Drain the water chestnuts, dry on kitchen paper and dust with cornflour.

❺ Arrange the ribs, pork cubes, chestnuts, spring rolls, chicken wings and vegetables on separate dishes.

❻ Heat the oil in a fondue pot until bubbling and serve. Guests start with spring rolls, then ribs, then dip pork cubes and water chestnuts into batter and cook, followed by chicken wings.

Preparation time: 20 minutes

Indian Extravaganza

Serve with Hot Curry Sauce (page 132), Cucumber and Mint
Sauce (page 138), lime pickles, mango chutney and lots of
warm naan bread and poppadums.

SERVES 6

INGREDIENTS	METRIC	IMPERIAL	AMERICAN
Chicken breast fillet, cut in			
strips	*225 g*	*8 oz*	*2 cups*
Plain yoghurt	*30 ml*	*2 tbsp*	*2 tbsp*
Garlic clove, crushed	*1*	*1*	*1*
Tandoori powder	*5–10 ml*	*1–2 tsp*	*1–2 tsp*
Salt and freshly ground			
black pepper			
Fiery Lamb Fondue (page 64)			
Ready-to-cook onion			
bahjias	*6*	*6*	*6*
Ready-to-cook samosas	*6*	*6*	*6*
Oil for fondue cooking			

METHOD

❶ Marinate the chicken with the yoghurt, garlic, tandoori
powder and salt and pepper in the fridge for at least
2 hours.

❷ Prepare the Lamb Fondue (see recipe) and arrange on a
serving plate. Drain the chicken and place on a separate
plate. Arrange the bahjias and samosas on another plate.

❸ Heat the oil in a fondue pot until bubbling. Serve
bahjias, then samosas, then finally chicken and lamb.

Preparation time: 20 minutes plus marinating

Fondue for Connoisseurs

Serve Sweet Spicy Sauce (page 136), Cranberry Relish (page 135), Fines Herbes Sauce (page 129), and Mustard Sauce (page 131) with this out-of-this-world fondue.

SERVES 4

INGREDIENTS	METRIC	IMPERIAL	AMERICAN
Hare fillet slices, cubed	*8-12*	*8-12*	*8-12*
Thin lamb chops, trimmed of fat	*8-12*	*8-12*	*8-12*
Olive oil	*250 ml*	*8 fl oz*	*1 cup*
Good pinch of salt			
Clear honey	*30 ml*	*2 tbsp*	*2 tbsp*
Red wine vinegar	*15 ml*	*1 tbsp*	*1 tbsp*
Garlic clove, crushed	*1*	*1*	*1*
Grated rind of ¹/₂ lemon			
Coarse ground peppercorns	*5 ml*	*1 tsp*	*1 tsp*
Crushed juniper berries	*5 ml*	*1 tsp*	*1 tsp*
Dried marjoram	*2.5 ml*	*¹/₂ tsp*	*¹/₂ tsp*
Dried thyme	*2.5 ml*	*¹/₂ tsp*	*¹/₂ tsp*
Oil for fondue cooking			

METHOD

❶ Put the meat in a bowl.

❷ Mix the remaining ingredients together except the oil for cooking and pour over. Toss well and leave to marinate in the fridge for at least 6 hours or overnight.

❸ Arrange the meat on serving dishes.

❹ Heat the oil in a fondue pot until bubbling and serve.

Preparation time: 20 minutes

Indonesian Kebab Fondue

Serve with Hot Curry Sauce (page 132), Chinese Garlic Sauce (page 128), plus the peanut sauce given in the recipe.

SERVES 4

INGREDIENTS	METRIC	IMPERIAL	AMERICAN
Pork fillet, cubed	225 g	8 oz	2 cups
Chicken breast fillet, cubed	225 g	8 oz	2 cups
Duck breast fillet, cubed	225 g	8 oz	2 cups
Lobster tails or scampi	8-12	8-12	8-12
Small pineapple, peeled and cubed	1	1	1
Banana, cut in chunks	1	1	1
Large onion, cut in wedges	1	1	1
Courgettes (zucchini), thickly sliced	2	2	2
Button mushrooms	225 g	8 oz	2 cups
Dry sherry	250 ml	8 fl oz	1 cup
Olive oil	120 ml	4 fl oz	1/2 cup
Cider vinegar	120 ml	4 fl oz	1/2 cup
Garlic cloves, chopped	2	2	2
Paprika	5 ml	1 tsp	1 tsp
Grated fresh root ginger	10 ml	2 tsp	2 tsp
For the peanut sauce			
Peanut butter	225 g	8 oz	1 cup
Cayenne	5 ml	1 tsp	1 tsp
Chicken stock	250 ml	8 fl oz	1 cup
Cornflour (cornstarch)	5-10 ml	1-2 tsp	1-2 tsp
Few drops of soy sauce			
Oil for fondue cooking			

METHOD

❶ Thread the meat, lobster, fruit and vegetables alternately on wooden skewers. Place in a shallow dish.

2 Mix the sherry, oil, vinegar, garlic, paprika and ginger together and pour over the kebabs.

3 Leave to marinate in the fridge for at least 1 hour (preferably a little longer), turning occasionally.

4 Make the sauce. Blend the peanut butter with the cayenne and stock in a saucepan and bring slowly to the boil. Mix the cornflour with a little water, stir in and simmer for 2 minutes, stirring. Flavour with soy sauce. Turn into a serving dish.

5 Arrange the kebabs on individual serving plates. Heat the oil in a fondue pot until bubbling. Serve.

Preparation time: 20 minutes plus marinating

Crispy Speciality Fondue

This is a substantial fondue with wonderful textures and flavours. Serve with Cocktail Sauce (page 124), Herb Cream (page 127), Peppercorn Sauce (page 130) and tartare sauce.

SERVES 4–6

INGREDIENTS	METRIC	IMPERIAL	AMERICAN
Broccoli florets	*100 g*	*4 oz*	*1 cup*
Cauliflower florets	*100 g*	*4 oz*	*1 cup*
Brussels sprouts, trimmed	*100g*	*4 oz*	*1 cup*
Carrots, diced	*100 g*	*4 oz*	*1 cup*
Pork fillet, cubed	*225 g*	*8 oz*	*2 cups*
Fillet steak, cubed	*225 g*	*8 oz*	*2 cups*
Lamb fillet, cubed	*225 g*	*8 oz*	*2 cups*
Garlic cloves, crushed	*2*	*2*	*2*
Salt	*5 ml*	*1 tsp*	*1 tsp*
Olive oil	*250 ml*	*8 fl oz*	*1 cup*
Onion, grated	*1*	*1*	*1*
Green peppercorns	*10 ml*	*2 tsp*	*2 tsp*
Dried mixed herbs	*10 ml*	*2 tsp*	*2 tsp*
For the batter			
Plain (all-purpose) flour	*250 g*	*9 oz*	*2¹/₄ cups*
Pinch of salt			
Milk	*250 ml*	*8 fl oz*	*1 cup*
Eggs, separated	*2*	*2*	*2*
Grated rind ¹/₂ lemon			
Oil for fondue cooking			

METHOD

❶ Cook the vegetables in boiling water for 5 minutes. Drain, rinse with cold water and dry on kitchen paper.

❷ Put the meat in a bowl.

❸ Mix the garlic, salt, oil, onion, peppercorns and herbs together. Pour over the meat and toss well. Leave to marinate in the fridge for at least 4 hours.

❹ Make the batter. Sift the flour and salt in a bowl. Add the milk, egg yolks and lemon rind and beat until smooth. When ready to serve whisk the egg whites until stiff and fold in with a metal spoon.

❺ Arrange the meats and vegetables on serving plates with a small dish of batter on each plate.

❻ Heat the oil in a fondue pot until bubbling. Guests dip a piece of food at a time into the batter and cook until crisp and golden.

Preparation time: 20 minutes plus marinating

Chop Suey Fondue

Another fabulous fondue from the Orient. Serve with Sweet Spicy Sauce (page 136), Chinese Garlic Sauce (page 128), Ginger Sauce (page 137), Caviar Sauce (page 125) and, of course, soy sauce.

Note: You really do need Chinese wire frying baskets to cook the food in the stock.

SERVES 4–6

INGREDIENTS	METRIC	IMPERIAL	AMERICAN
Fillet steak, cut in thin strips	*100 g*	*4 oz*	*1 cup*
Veal fillet, cut in strips	*100 g*	*4 oz*	*1 cup*
Duck breast fillet, cut in strips	*100 g*	*4 oz*	*1 cup*
Calves' or lambs' liver, cut in strips	*100 g*	*4 oz*	*1 cup*
Lambs' kidneys, cut in slices	*100 g*	*4 oz*	*1 cup*
Mushrooms, sliced	*100 g*	*4 oz*	*2 cups*
Carrots, cut in matchsticks	*100 g*	*4 oz*	*1 cup*
Broccoli florets, plunged in boiling water, drained and rinsed with cold water	*100 g*	*4 oz*	*1 cup*
Swede (rutabaga), cut in matchsticks	*100 g*	*4 oz*	*1 cup*
Beansprouts	*100 g*	*4 oz*	*1 cup*
Chicken stock	*1 L*	*1³/₄ pts*	*4¹/₄ cups*
Garlic clove, chopped	*1*	*1*	*1*
Grated fresh root ginger	*10 ml*	*2 tsp*	*2 tsp*
Cider vinegar	*120 ml*	*4 fl oz*	*¹/₂ cup*
Soy sauce	*120 ml*	*4 fl oz*	*¹/₂ cup*
Clear honey	*20 ml*	*4 tsp*	*4 tsp*

METHOD

❶ Arrange the meats and vegetables attractively on serving plates.

❷ Put the remaining ingredients in a fondue pot or a saucepan and simmer for 8 minutes. Transfer to a fondue pot, if necessary, and place on the table. Serve.

Preparation time: 15 minutes

Hong Kong Hilton!

Side dishes of soy sauce and chopped cashew nuts are all that's needed to complete this fondue, plus, perhaps a dish of rice crackers to nibble.

SERVES 4

INGREDIENTS	METRIC	IMPERIAL	AMERICAN
Pork fillet, cut in strips	350 g	12 oz	3 cups
Pigs' liver, cut in thin slices	350 g	12 oz	3 cups
Red (bell) pepper, cut in chunks	1	1	1
Green (bell) pepper, cut in chunks	1	1	1
Bunch of spring onions (scallions), trimmed and cut in pieces			
Swede (rutabaga), diced	100 g	4 oz	1 cup
Fresh peeled, or canned lychees	100 g	4 oz	1 cup
Fresh or canned pineapple, cubed	100 g	4 oz	1 cup
Fresh or canned mango, cubed	100 g	4 oz	1 cup
Beef stock	500 ml	17 fl oz	2^1/$_2$ cups
Soy sauce	120 ml	4 fl oz	^{1}/$_2$ cup
Rice (or dry white) wine	250 ml	8 fl oz	1 cup
Tomato purée (paste)	15 ml	1 tbsp	1 tbsp
Clear honey	15 ml	1 tbsp	1 tbsp
Oyster sauce	60 ml	4 tbsp	4 tbsp
Pinch of saffron powder			

METHOD

❶ Arrange the meat, vegetables and fruit attractively on serving plates.

❷ Put the remaining ingredients in a fondue pot or a saucepan and simmer for 8 minutes. Transfer to a fondue pot, if necessary, and place on the table.

❸ Serve, using frying baskets to cook the food in the stock.

Preparation time: 15 minutes

Mongolian Munch

Spicy, succulent, exciting are the best ways of describing this fondue. Serve with Hot Curry Sauce (page 132), Whipped Pineapple Sauce (page 121) and a bowl of plain yoghurt flavoured with snipped chives and a little salt and pepper.

SERVES 4

INGREDIENTS	METRIC	IMPERIAL	AMERICAN
Goose breast fillet, cut in strips	175 g	6 oz	1^1/$_2$ cups
Duck breast fillet, cut in strips	175 g	6 oz	1^1/$_2$ cups
Pork fillet, cut in strips	175 g	6 oz	1^1/$_2$ cups
Bamboo shoots	100 g	4 oz	1 cup
Broccoli florets, blanched for 2 minutes, drained and rinsed with cold water	100 g	4 oz	1 cup
Transparent noodles, cooked	200 g	7 oz	1^3/$_4$ cups
Chicken stock	750 ml	1^1/$_4$ pts	3 cups
Hoisin sauce	120 ml	4 fl oz	^{1}/$_2$ cup
Garlic cloves, chopped	2	2	2
Medium sherry	250 ml	8 fl oz	1 cup
Cider vinegar	120 ml	4 fl oz	^{1}/$_2$ cup
Small red chilli, seeded and chopped			
Salt and freshly ground black pepper			

METHOD

❶ Arrange the meat and vegetables with the noodles on individual serving dishes.

❷ Put the remaining ingredients in a fondue pot or a saucepan. Simmer for 8 minutes. Transfer to a fondue pot, if necessary, and place on the table.

❸ Serve, using wire baskets to cook the food.

Preparation time: 20 minutes

Christmas Fondue

For a traditional feel to the meal, serve with boiled, skinned chestnuts and lightly cooked baby Brussels sprouts, plus Potato Skins (page 117). Add a dish of roast potatoes for good measure!

SERVES 6

INGREDIENTS	METRIC	IMPERIAL	AMERICAN
Chicken stock	*450 ml*	*³/₄ pt*	*2 cups*
Turkey breast fillets	*4-6*	*4-6*	*4-6*
Peppercorns	*6*	*6*	*6*
Garlic clove, crushed	*1*	*1*	*1*
Fresh cranberries	*450 g*	*1 lb*	*4 cups*
Caster (superfine) sugar	*275 g*	*10 oz*	*1¹/₄ cups*
Port	*30 ml*	*2 tbsp*	*2 tbsp*

METHOD

❶ Put the stock in a large saucepan, bring to the boil and add the turkey breasts, peppercorns and garlic. Lower the heat and poach the turkey breast for approximately 20 minutes until tender.

❷ Put the cranberries, sugar and 450 ml/³/₄ pt/2 cups water in a saucepan. Heat gently, stirring all the time, until the sugar has dissolved. Boil for 5 minutes and stir in the port. Lower the heat and simmer for 10 minutes.

❸ Drain the turkey, allow to cool and chop into small chunks. Serve with the cranberry sauce served in the fondue pot over a very low heat.

Preparation time: 35 minutes

Vegetable Fondues

These are delicious on their own after a cheese fondue or are the perfect accompaniment to a simple meat-cooked-in-oil with sauces fondue.

Spicy Cumin Balls

Serve with Hot Curry Sauce (page 132), Cucumber and Mint Sauce (page 138) and mango chutney.

SERVES 6

INGREDIENTS	METRIC	IMPERIAL	AMERICAN
Bulgar wheat	*100g*	*4oz*	*³/₄ cup*
Boiling water	*90 ml*	*6 tbsp*	*6 tbsp*
Canned chick peas			
(garbanzos), drained	*2 x 425 g*	*2 x 15 oz*	*2 large cans*
Oil	*30 ml*	*2 tbsp*	*2 tbsp*
Garlic cloves, crushed	*2*	*2*	*2*
Chilli powder	*5 ml*	*1 tsp*	*1 tsp*
Ground cumin	*5 ml*	*1 tsp*	*1 tsp*
Oil for fondue cooking			

METHOD

❶ Put the bulgar wheat into a bowl and pour over the boiling water. Allow to soak for 1 hour.

❷ Place the chick peas in a processor with the bulgar wheat and the remaining ingredients except the cooking oil.

❸ Blend for 2 minutes until the mixture is smooth.

❹ Mould the mixture into small balls and place on a serving dish.

❺ Heat the oil in a fondue pot until bubbling and serve.

Preparation time: 10 minutes plus soaking

Herby Potato Balls

Delicious to accompany any meat or fish fondue or to serve as a starter with Cocktail Sauce (page 124) and Herb Cream (page 127).

SERVES 4

INGREDIENTS	METRIC	IMPERIAL	AMERICAN
Mashed potatoes	*900 g*	*2 lb*	*4 cups*
Brussels sprouts	*225 g*	*8 oz*	*2 cups*
Dry mustard	*5 ml*	*1 tsp*	*1 tsp*
Garlic clove, crushed	*1*	*1*	*1*
Salt and freshly ground black pepper			
Eggs, beaten	*2*	*2*	*2*
Chopped parsley	*30 ml*	*2 tbsp*	*2 tbsp*
Chopped thyme	*30 ml*	*2 tbsp*	*2 tbsp*
Oil for fondue cooking			

METHOD

❶ Blend the mashed potatoes and Brussels sprouts together and add the mustard and crushed garlic.

❷ Season the mixture with the salt and pepper and form into small balls.

❸ Place the beaten eggs on a flat dish and mix the herbs in a shallow dish. Roll each potato ball in the egg and then in the chopped herbs. Repeat the process again and pile the balls on a serving dish.

❹ Heat the oil in a fondue pot, until bubbling. Serve.

Preparation time: 15 minutes

Bean and Sweetcorn Fondue

This fondue can be used as a cold dip for parties. Serve with vegetable dippers and tortilla chips. Use two drained cans of beans instead of cooking your own if you prefer.

SERVES 6

INGREDIENTS	METRIC	IMPERIAL	AMERICAN
Black-eyed beans (soaked overnight in cold water)	225 g	8 oz	1¹/₃ cups
Frozen sweetcorn (corn)	450 g	1lb	4 cups
Onion, chopped	1	1	1
Tabasco sauce	2.5 ml	¹/₂ tsp	¹/₂ tsp
Curry paste	2.5 ml	¹/₂ tsp	¹/₂ tsp
Garlic clove, crushed	1	1	1
Cornflour (cornstarch)	30 ml	2 tbsp	2 tbsp
Medium sherry	30 ml	2 tbsp	2 tbsp
Single (light) cream	45 ml	3 tbsp	3 tbsp

METHOD

❶ Add enough fresh water to cover the beans, bring to the boil, boil rapidly for 10 minutes, then simmer for 1 hour or until the beans are tender. Drain. Alternatively, use drained canned black-eyed beans.

❷ Put the sweetcorn into a saucepan with 30 ml/2 tbsp water and simmer for 8 minutes until tender.

❸ Place the corn and its liquid into a blender. Add the onion and drained black-eyed beans and process until soft.

❹ Stir the Tabasco sauce, curry paste and crushed garlic into the purée.

5 Mix the cornflour with the sherry and mix into the purée with the cream.

6 Put the mixture into a fondue pot and heat very gently, stirring frequently. Serve when piping hot.

Preparation time: 1¹/₂ hours (less if using canned beans)

Mushroom Fondue

If you are really ambitious, choose a selection of different mushrooms. Serve with Cheese and Onion Sauce (page 139), Red Pepper Sauce (page 134) and for Cocktail Sauce (page 124). Follow with a cheese board and crusty bread.

SERVES 4

INGREDIENTS	METRIC	IMPERIAL	AMERICAN
Cornflour (cornstarch)	*30-45 ml*	*2-3 tbsp*	*2-3 tbsp*
Paprika	*10 ml*	*2 tsp*	*2 tsp*
Salt and freshly ground black pepper			
Button mushrooms,	*350 g*	*12 oz*	*3 cups*
Oil for fondue cooking			

METHOD

1 Mix the cornflour, paprika and salt and pepper together and toss the mushrooms in the mixture.

2 Arrange on individual plates.

3 Heat the oil in a fondue pot until bubbling. Spear mushrooms and cook until lightly golden.

Preparation time: 5 minutes

Vegetable Kebab Fondue

The kebabs can be cooked then served with any cheese fondue (pages 11–27) or an oriental sauce (see page 120).

SERVES 4

INGREDIENTS	METRIC	IMPERIAL	AMERICAN
Eggs	2	2	2
Plain (all-purpose) flour	100 g	4 oz	1 cup
Water	250 ml	8 fl oz	1 cup
Courgettes (zucchini), cut into chunks	2	2	2
Button mushrooms	16	16	16
Cherry tomatoes	8	8	8
Red (bell) pepper, cut into chunks	1	1	1
Green (bell) pepper, cut into chunks	1	1	1
Oil for fondue cooking			

METHOD

❶ Make the batter by beating the eggs and flour together in a bowl and blending in the water. Beat for 5 minutes until frothy.

❷ Thread the vegetables onto skewers and place two at each serving.

❸ Heat the oil in a fondue pot until bubbling. Each person dips the skewered vegetables into the batter and then into the hot oil until the batter is crisp and golden. Serve with small bowls of rice.

Preparation time: 15 minutes

New Potatoes and Artichoke Fondue

The addition of the lemon juice to the Jerusalem artichokes prevents them from turning brown.

SERVES 4–6

INGREDIENTS	METRIC	IMPERIAL	AMERICAN
Baby new potatoes, scrubbed	750 g	1¹/₂ lb	6 cups
Salt	5 ml	1 tsp	1 tsp
Jerusalem artichokes, scrubbed and cut in chunks	275 g	10 oz	2¹/₂ cups
Lemon juice	5 ml	1 tsp	1 tsp
Oil for fondue cooking			

METHOD

❶ Place the potatoes in a saucepan of water with the salt. Bring to the boil and cook for 10 minutes until just cooked but not soft. Drain, rinse in cold water and drain again. Place in a bowl.

❷ Put the artichokes in a pan of water with the lemon juice. Bring to the boil and cook for 6 minutes. Drain, rinse with cold water and drain. Place in a bowl.

❸ Heat the oil in a fondue pot until bubbling. Each person dips the potatoes and artichokes in the oil with a fondue fork or Chinese wire strainer and fries them until crisp and golden.

Preparation time: 20 minutes

Vegetable and Tomato Fondue

Serve this fondue with small cooked new potatoes and cubes of cheese.

SERVES 4–6

INGREDIENTS	METRIC	IMPERIAL	AMERICAN
Butter	50 g	2 oz	1/4 cup
Large onion, chopped	1	1	1
Carrots, chopped	275 g	10 oz	2 1/2 cups
Small swede (rutabaga), chopped	1	1	1
Small turnip, chopped	1	1	1
Tomatoes, skinned and chopped	4	4	4
Chicken stock	250 ml	8 fl oz	1 cup
Salt and freshly ground black pepper			
Pinch of cayenne			

METHOD

1 Melt the butter in a saucepan and fry (sauté) the onion until soft but not brown. Add the rest of the chopped vegetables, the tomatoes and stock.

2 Bring to the boil, cover and simmer for 20 minutes until the vegetables are tender. Drain, reserving the stock and allow to cool for 2 minutes.

3 Purée the vegetables in a blender. Stir in the salt and pepper and cayenne. Thin with a little stock if necessary.

VEGETABLE FONDUES

❹ Pour the purée into a fondue pot over a low heat and serve.

Preparation time: 15 minutes

Potato Skins

Great to serve with Christmas Fondue (page 106).

SERVES 4

INGREDIENTS	METRIC	IMPERIAL	AMERICAN
Even-sized potatoes	*1.5 kg*	*3 lb*	*3 lb*
Butter, melted	*75 g*	*3 oz*	*$^1/_3$ cup*
Salt			

METHOD

❶ Scrub the potatoes and prick with a fork. Bake in the oven at 200°C/400°F/gas mark 6 for 1 hour or until they are tender, or microwave according to your microwave instructions.

❷ Remove the potatoes from the oven or microwave and cut each into quarters. Remove the soft potato from the inside of the skin and save for topping shepherd's pie or for Herby Potato Balls (page 109).

❸ Brush the potato skins on both sides with the melted butter and place on a baking sheet. Put in the oven for 6–8 minutes until they are crisp and brown at the edges. Serve with any rich fondue dipping sauce.

Preparation time: 1$^1/_2$ hours (less if you microwave the potatoes)

Crispy Fried Mushrooms

Serve the mushrooms with Cheese and Onion Sauce (page 139) or tartare sauce.

SERVES 3

INGREDIENTS	METRIC	IMPERIAL	AMERICAN
Button mushrooms	350 g	12 oz	3 cups
Fresh white breadcrumbs	100 g	4 oz	2 cups
Eggs	2	2	2
Chopped parsley	15 ml	1 tbsp	1 tbsp
Ground cumin	5 ml	1 tsp	1 tsp
Ground coriander (cilantro)	5 ml	1 tsp	1 tsp
Salt	2.5 ml	1/2 tsp	1/2 tsp
Oil for fondue cooking			

METHOD

❶ Trim the mushrooms.

❷ Beat the eggs together in a shallow dish.

❸ Mix together the breadcrumbs, parsley, cumin, coriander and salt on a plate.

❹ Dip the mushrooms first in the egg and then in the breadcrumb mixture. Repeat the process until the mushrooms are completely coated. Set aside until ready to serve. Arrange on serving plates.

❺ Heat the oil in a fondue pot until bubbling. Serve.

Preparation time: 10 minutes

Pimiento Fondue

A rich, spicy fondue perfect for serving with deep-fried potato skins and small skewers of vegetables.

SERVES 4

INGREDIENTS	METRIC	IMPERIAL	AMERICAN
Butter	*50 g*	*2 oz*	*¹/₄ cup*
Onion, finely chopped	*1*	*1*	*1*
Very ripe tomatoes,			
* skinned and chopped*	*450 g*	*1 lb*	*4 cups*
Garlic cloves, crushed	*2*	*2*	*2*
Can pimientos, drained			
* and chopped*	*175 g*	*6 oz*	*1 small can*
Salt and freshly ground			
* black pepper*			
Soy sauce	*5 ml*	*1 tsp*	*1 tsp*

METHOD

❶ Melt the butter in a fondue pot and add the onion. Cook until soft but not brown and stir in the crushed garlic.

❷ Add the tomatoes to the onion and garlic and cook for 10 minutes, stirring frequently. Reduce the heat.

❸ Season the tomatoes with the salt and pepper and stir in the chopped pimientos and soy sauce. Serve.

Preparation time: 15 minutes

Sauces and Dips

Most fish and meat fondues need extra-special dips and sauces to make them memorable. Here is a selection which will fit the bill perfectly.

Whipped Pineapple Sauce

Apart from being used as recommended, this sauce is ideal with plain pork or chicken fondues.

SERVES 4

INGREDIENTS	METRIC	IMPERIAL	AMERICAN
Crème fraîche	150 ml	1/4 pt	2/3 cup
Slices of canned or fresh pineapple, puréed	2	2	2
Lemon juice	2.5 ml	1/2 tsp	1/2 tsp
Rum	2.5 ml	1/2 tsp	1/2 tsp
Salt and freshly ground black pepper			
Good pinch of cayenne			

METHOD

❶ Put all the ingredients in a bowl. Whisk thoroughly until frothy.

❷ Chill until ready to serve.

Preparation time: 5 minutes plus chilling

Sweet and Sour Sauce

Serve with any pork or poultry fondues.

SERVES 4-6

INGREDIENTS	METRIC	IMPERIAL	AMERICAN
Cornflour (cornstarch)	10 ml	2 tsp	2 tsp
Malt vinegar	15 ml	1 tbsp	1 tbsp
Can crushed pineapple	240 g	8 ³/₄ oz	1 small can
Tomato ketchup (catsup)	30 ml	2 tbsp	2 tbsp
Soy sauce	15 ml	1 tbsp	1 tbsp
Small cucumber, finely diced	¹/₄	¹/₄	¹/₄

METHOD

❶ Blend the cornflour with the vinegar in a small pan.

❷ Stir in the remaining ingredients, bring to the boil and simmer for 5 minutes. Serve warm.

Preparation time: 10 minutes

Rouille

Rich and garlicky, this sauce is ideal for fish and meat fondues.

SERVES 4

INGREDIENTS	METRIC	IMPERIAL	AMERICAN
Slice of white bread, crusts removed	*1*	*1*	*1*
Red chilli, seeded and chopped	*1*	*1*	*1*
Small red (bell) pepper, chopped	*1*	*1*	*1*
Garlic cloves, chopped	*2*	*2*	*2*
Egg yolk	*1*	*1*	*1*
Olive oil	*150 ml*	*¹/₄ pt*	*²/₃ cup*
Salt			

METHOD

❶ Soak the bread in water then squeeze dry and place in a blender or food processor.

❷ Run the machine and drop in the chilli, red pepper, garlic and egg yolk.

❸ With the machine running, add the oil a drop at a time until the mixture is thick and glossy, like mayonnaise.

❹ Season with salt and serve.

Preparation time: 10 minutes

Cocktail Sauce

Serve with white meat or fish fondues.

SERVES 4

INGREDIENTS	METRIC	IMPERIAL	AMERICAN
Mayonnaise	*250 ml*	*8 fl oz*	*1 cup*
Plain yoghurt	*150 ml*	*¼ pt*	*⅔ cup*
Redcurrant jelly (clear conserve), melted	*20 ml*	*4 tsp*	*4 tsp*
Tomato ketchup (catsup)	*20 ml*	*4 tsp*	*4 tsp*
Curry powder or paste	*5 ml*	*1 tsp*	*1 tsp*
Salt and freshly ground black pepper			
Pinch of cayenne			
Few drops of lemon juice (optional)			

METHOD

❶ Blend the mayonnaise and yoghurt together.

❷ Whisk in the redcurrant jelly, ketchup and curry powder or paste.

❸ Season with salt, pepper and cayenne, then add a little lemon juice, if necessary, to sharpen the flavour.

Preparation time: 10 minutes

Caviar Sauce

Serve with luxurious fish and seafood fondues. But the saltiness of the 'caviar' goes surprisingly well with game and red meat too.

SERVES 4

INGREDIENTS	METRIC	IMPERIAL	AMERICAN
Thick Greek-style yoghurt	*150 ml*	*¼ pt*	*⅔ cup*
Juice of ½ lemon			
Clear honey	*10 ml*	*2 tsp*	*2 tsp*
Sherry	*2.5 ml*	*½ tsp*	*½ tsp*
Freshly ground black pepper			
Pinch of cayenne			
Red or black Danish lumpfish roe (mock caviar)	*45 ml*	*3 tbsp*	*3 tbsp*

METHOD

❶ Mix the yoghurt with the lemon juice and honey.

❷ Add the sherry then season with pepper and cayenne.

❸ Stir in the lumpfish roe just before serving.

Preparation time: 10 minutes

Dill Cream

Delicious with fish but good with any meat or poultry fondue too.

SERVES 4

INGREDIENTS	METRIC	IMPERIAL	AMERICAN
Soured (dairy sour) cream	150 ml	1/4 pt	2/3 cup
Juice of 1/2 lemon			
Few drops of Worcestershire sauce			
Salt and freshly ground black pepper			
Pinch of caster (superfine) sugar			
Chopped dill (dillweed)	30 ml	2 tbsp	2 tbsp
Brandy	2.5 ml	1/2 tsp	1/2 tsp

METHOD

❶ Whisk all the ingredients except the brandy together in a bowl. Chill.

❷ Just before serving, stir in the brandy.

Preparation time: 5 minutes plus chilling

Herb Cream

Ring the changes with different herbs to blend with the type of meat you are serving: try rosemary and mint with lamb, sage and parsley with pork, thyme instead of oregano for poultry.

SERVES 4

INGREDIENTS	METRIC	IMPERIAL	AMERICAN
Mayonnaise	250 ml	8 fl oz	1 cup
Crème fraîche	250 ml	8 fl oz	1 cup
Juice of 1 lemon			
Chopped parsley	15 ml	1 tbsp	1 tbsp
Snipped chives	15 ml	1 tbsp	1 tbsp
Chopped marjoram or oregano	15 ml	1 tbsp	1 tbsp
Few drops of Worcestershire sauce			
Pinch of caster (superfine) sugar			
Salt and freshly ground black pepper			

METHOD

❶ Whisk the mayonnaise, crème fraîche and lemon juice in a bowl until frothy.

❷ Fold in the herbs and season with Worcestershire sauce, sugar, salt and pepper to taste. Chill until ready to serve.

Preparation time: 5 minutes plus chilling

Chinese Garlic Sauce

Obviously oriental, this sauce is lovely with all types of meat, poultry or fish.

SERVES 4

INGREDIENTS	METRIC	IMPERIAL	AMERICAN
Garlic cloves	4	4	4
Salt	5 ml	1 tsp	1 tsp
Handful of parsley, chopped			
Handful of chives, snipped			
Clear honey	20 ml	4 tsp	4 tsp
Juice of 1 lemon			
Dry sherry or rice wine	250 ml	8 fl oz	1 cup
Soy sauce	20 ml	4 tsp	4 tsp
Sesame or sunflower oil	20 ml	4 tsp	4 tsp
Hard-boiled (hard-cooked) eggs, finely chopped	2	2	2
Salt and freshly ground black pepper			

METHOD

❶ Crush the garlic with the salt. Put in a bowl and blend in the herbs, honey, lemon juice, sherry and soy sauce.

❷ Beat in the oil, a drop at a time.

❸ Fold in the eggs and season with salt and pepper.

Preparation time: 10 minutes

Fines Herbes Sauce

A light elegant sauce for more delicate meats and fish.

SERVES 4

INGREDIENTS	METRIC	IMPERIAL	AMERICAN
Medium-dry white wine	250 ml	8 fl oz	1 cup
Olive oil	20 ml	4 tsp	4 tsp
Wine vinegar	20 ml	4 tsp	4 tsp
Chopped parsley	15 ml	1 tbsp	1 tbsp
Snipped chives	15 ml	1 tbsp	1 tbsp
Chopped lemon balm or oregano	15 ml	1 tbsp	1 tbsp
Garlic cloves, finely chopped	2	2	2
French mustard	10 ml	2 tsp	2 tsp
Hard-boiled (hard-cooked) egg, finely chopped	1	1	1
Salt and freshly ground black pepper			

METHOD

❶ Whisk the wine with the oil, vinegar, herbs, garlic and mustard.

❷ Stir in the egg and season to taste with salt and pepper.

Preparation time: 5 minutes

Peppercorn Sauce

A delicious combination which goes very well with red meats.

SERVES 4

INGREDIENTS	METRIC	IMPERIAL	AMERICAN
Mayonnaise	250 ml	8 fl oz	1 cup
Plain yoghurt	150 ml	¹/₄ pt	²/₃ cup
Juice of ¹/₂ lemon			
Redcurrant jelly (clear conserve), melted	30 ml	2 tbsp	2 tbsp
Pickled green or pink peppercorns, drained	20 ml	4 tsp	4 tsp
Brandy	2.5 ml	¹/₂ tsp	¹/₂ tsp
Chopped parsley	15 ml	1 tbsp	1 tbsp
Snipped chives	15 ml	1 tbsp	1 tbsp

METHOD

❶ Blend the mayonnaise with the yoghurt, lemon juice and redcurrant jelly.

❷ Stir in the peppercorns and remaining ingredients.

❸ Chill before serving.

Preparation time: 5 minutes plus chilling

Mustard Sauce

Very different from the English-style flavoured white sauce, this goes exceptionally well with red meats and oily fish.

SERVES 4

INGREDIENTS	METRIC	IMPERIAL	AMERICAN
Greek-style yoghurt	250 ml	8 fl oz	1 cup
Mayonnaise	250 ml	8 fl oz	1 cup
English mustard	15 ml	1 tbsp	1 tbsp
Juice of $1/2$ lemon			
Few drops of Worcestershire sauce			
Pinch of caster (superfine) sugar			
Salt and freshly ground black pepper			
Snipped chives	30 ml	2 tbsp	2 tbsp

METHOD

❶ Blend the yoghurt with the mayonnaise, mustard and lemon juice.

❷ Season with Worcestershire sauce, sugar, salt and pepper to taste and fold in the chives. Chill, if time, before serving.

Preparation time: 5 minutes plus chilling

Hot Curry Sauce

A fiery blend to complement any meat or poultry fondue.

SERVES 4–6

INGREDIENTS	METRIC	IMPERIAL	AMERICAN
Sunflower or olive oil	15 ml	1 tbsp	1 tbsp
Onion, finely chopped	1	1	1
Hot curry powder or paste	10 ml	2 tsp	2 tsp
Cornflour (cornstarch)	15 ml	1 tbsp	1 tbsp
Milk	300 ml	1/2 pt	1¹/₄ cups
Coconut milk	150 ml	1/4 pt	²/₃ cup

METHOD

❶ Heat the oil in a saucepan, add the onion and cook, stirring, until soft but not brown.

❷ Stir in the curry powder and cook for 2 minutes.

❸ Blend the cornflour with the milk and stir into the curry and onion. Pour in the coconut milk and continue cooking, stirring all the time until the sauce thickens. Serve hot.

Preparation time: 5 minutes

Garlic Sauce

A light yet pungent dipping sauce, good with most meats or fish.

SERVES 4

INGREDIENTS	METRIC	IMPERIAL	AMERICAN
Fresh breadcrumbs	*100 g*	*4 oz*	*2 cups*
Garlic cloves	*3*	*3*	*3*
Lemon juice	*15 ml*	*1 tbsp*	*1 tbsp*
Vinegar	*15 ml*	*1 tbsp*	*1 tbsp*
Olive oil	*250 ml*	*8 fl oz*	*1 cup*
Plain yoghurt	*75 ml*	*5 tbsp*	*5 tbsp*
Salt and freshly ground black pepper			

METHOD

❶ Put the breadcrumbs in a blender or processor with the garlic, lemon juice and vinegar and blend well together.

❷ Add the oil a little at a time and process until a smooth mixture has formed.

❸ Blend in the yoghurt and season with the salt and pepper. Chill until ready to serve.

Preparation time: 5 minutes plus chilling

Red Pepper Sauce

Serve this colourful sauce with poultry, fish or meat for the perfect accompaniment.

SERVES 4–6

INGREDIENTS	METRIC	IMPERIAL	AMERICAN
Butter	25 g	1 oz	2 tbsp
Large onion, chopped	1	1	1
Red (bell) peppers, chopped	2	2	2
Garlic clove, crushed	1	1	1
Chicken stock	300 ml	1/2 pt	1 1/4 cups
Salt and freshly ground black pepper			

METHOD

❶ Melt the butter and fry (sauté) the chopped onion until soft but not brown. Stir in the red peppers and garlic.

❷ Cook gently for 5 minutes. Pour in the stock and season with the salt and pepper. Simmer for 15 minutes or until pulpy. Serve hot.

Preparation time: 10 minutes

Cranberry Relish

The sharp, tangy taste of the cranberries contrasts well with many poultry and meat fondues. Defrost frozen cranberries before use.

SERVES 6

INGREDIENTS	METRIC	IMPERIAL	AMERICAN
Fresh or frozen cranberries	*450 g*	*1 lb*	*4 cups*
Caster (superfine) sugar	*450 g*	*1 lb*	*2 cups*
Water	*250 ml*	*8 fl oz*	*1 cup*
Cinnamon	*5 ml*	*1 tsp*	*1 tsp*
Grated rind and juice of 1 orange			
Brandy	*30 ml*	*2 tbsp*	*2 tbsp*

METHOD

❶ Put the cranberries, sugar, water, cinnamon, orange rind and juice in a large saucepan and bring to the boil.

❷ Cover with a lid, reduce the heat and simmer for 20 minutes, stirring occasionally.

❸ Remove from the heat. Skim off any white foam from the top of the cranberry sauce. Stir in the brandy and serve warm.

Preparation time: 25 minutes

Sweet Spicy Sauce

A tangy combination that lends itself to pork or poultry in particular.

SERVES 4–6

INGREDIENTS	METRIC	IMPERIAL	AMERICAN
Olive oil	10 ml	2 tsp	2 tsp
Onion, finely chopped	1	1	1
Tomato purée (paste)	15 ml	1 tbsp	1 tbsp
Red wine vinegar	15 ml	1 tbsp	1 tbsp
Orange marmalade	60 ml	4 tbsp	4 tbsp
Golden (light corn) syrup	45 ml	3 tbsp	3 tbsp
Dry mustard	45 ml	3 tbsp	3 tbsp
Worcestershire sauce	15 ml	1 tbsp	1 tbsp
Cornflour (cornstarch)	15 ml	1 tbsp	1 tbsp
Chicken stock	450 ml	$^3/_4$ pt	2 cups

METHOD

❶ Heat the oil and fry (sauté) the onion until soft and lightly golden. Lower the heat and stir in the tomato purée, vinegar, marmalade, golden syrup, mustard and Worcestershire sauce.

❷ Blend the cornflour with a little of the stock and mix into the onion mixture. Pour in the rest of the stock and simmer for 10 minutes, stirring all the time. Combine with the first mixture and serve in the fondue pot, keeping the heat on low, or simply serve hot.

Preparation time: 20 minutes

Ginger Sauce

Another sauce from the Orient. Serve with any meat or fish.

SERVES 4

INGREDIENTS	METRIC	IMPERIAL	AMERICAN
Grated fresh ginger root	*20 ml*	*4 tsp*	*4 tsp*
Dry sherry	*45 ml*	*3 tbsp*	*3 tbsp*
Soy sauce	*30 ml*	*2 tbsp*	*2 tbsp*
Hot water	*45 ml*	*3 tbsp*	*3 tbsp*

METHOD

❶ Mix all the ingredients together. Serve in individual small bowls.

Preparation time: 5 minutes

Cucumber and Mint Sauce

A cool, refreshing sauce, delicious with lamb in particular.

SERVES 4–6

INGREDIENTS	METRIC	IMPERIAL	AMERICAN
Low fat soft cheese	*100 g*	*4 oz*	*¹/₂ cup*
Plain yoghurt	*150 ml*	*¹/₄ pt*	*²/₃ cup*
Cucumber, finely diced	*¹/₂*	*¹/₂*	*¹/₂*
Chopped mint	*30 ml*	*2 tbsp*	*2 tbsp*
Lemon juice	*10 ml*	*2 tsp*	*2 tsp*
Salt and freshly ground black pepper			

METHOD

❶ Beat the cheese and yoghurt together until smooth.

❷ Stir in the cucumber, mint and lemon juice and season with the salt and pepper. Serve chilled.

Preparation time: 5 minutes

Cheese and Onion Sauce

A simple sauce, good with any fondue. Try it as a topping for jacket potatoes too!

SERVES 4

INGREDIENTS	METRIC	IMPERIAL	AMERICAN
Low fat soft cheese	175 g	6 oz	$^3/_4$ cup
Soured (dairy sour) cream	75 ml	5 tbsp	5 tbsp
Bunch of spring onions (scallions), finely chopped	$^1/_2$	$^1/_2$	$^1/_2$
Pinch of cayenne			

METHOD

1 Blend all the ingredients together and serve chilled.

Preparation time: 5 minutes plus chilling

CHEAT SAUCES

Making your own sauces, dips and relishes is ideal, but don't be afraid to cheat. Jars of Hollondaise, Béarnaise and Poivre sauce are excellent as are some of the sweet and sour and barbecue sauces.

Containers of fresh dips (available at all good supermarkets) go down a treat with most people as do the jars of corn, tomato, chilli or cucumber relish.

The best thing of all to keep in your cupboard is a jar of good quality French mayonnaise. It can be flavoured with just about any store cupboard ingredient from cheese to garlic for a delicious dip.

Convenience Fondues

Here are some great ideas for fondues using ready-prepared convenience foods. They're quick, they're easy and most of all, they're delicious.

Russian Fondue

Serve with Red Pepper Sauce (page 134), rye bread and crisp lettuce.

SERVES 3–4

INGREDIENTS	METRIC	IMPERIAL	AMERICAN
Can mixed vegetables, *drained*	*425 g*	*15 oz*	*1 large* *can*
Mayonnaise	*30 ml*	*2 tbsp*	*2 tbsp*
Smoked pork ring	*1*	*1*	*1*
Packet (about 15) Mini *Kievs*	*1*	*1*	*1*
Oil for fondue cooking			

METHOD

❶ Make the Russian salad by mixing the can of vegetables with the mayonnaise. Chill until ready to serve.

❷ Cut the pork ring into bite-sized pieces. Arrange with the Kievs on individual plates.

❸ Heat the oil in a fondue pot until bubbling. Each diner spears a Kiev or piece of pork ring and cooks until golden. Then eats it with the cold Russian salad.

Preparation time: 5 minutes plus chilling

Hot Dog Fondue

Serve this fun fondue with ketchup (catsup) and Mustard
Sauce (page 131) or a selection of bought dips. Bite-sized
cubes of burger also make a good base for a fondue.

SERVES 4

INGREDIENTS	METRIC	IMPERIAL	AMERICAN
Can (8) hot dog sausages	400 g	14 oz	1 large can
Slices of bread from a large cut loaf	8	8	8
French mustard (optional)			
Oil for fondue cooking			

METHOD

❶ Drain the hot dog sausages and dry on kitchen paper.

❷ Cut the crusts off the bread then roll the slices flat with a
rolling pin. Spread with mustard, if liked.

❸ Roll a sausage up in each slice of bread. Cut in halves
and secure each half with a wooden cocktail stick
(toothpick).

❹ Heat the oil in a fondue pot until bubbling. Guests
spear a hot dog roll, and fry until the bread is golden.

Preparation time: 10 minutes

Chicken Maryland Fondue

Serve bought corn relish, a green salad and crusty bread with this fondue. For a party, you could have baby corn cobs to cook too.

SERVES 4

INGREDIENTS	METRIC	IMPERIAL	AMERICAN
Large bananas	2	2	2
Lemon juice			
Rashers (slices) streaky bacon	4 or 8	4 or 8	4 or 8
Chicken nuggets	16	16	16
Oil for fondue cooking			

METHOD

❶ Cut each banana into 6 bite-sized chunks. Toss in lemon juice to prevent browning.

❷ Discard any rind from the bacon, cut the rashers in half and roll up.

❸ Arrange the banana and bacon on individual plates with the chicken nuggets.

❹ Heat the oil in a fondue pot until bubbling. Guests fry chicken, bacon and banana a piece at a time in the pot and transfer them to their plates for eating.

Preparation time: 10 minutes

Tortellini Fondue

You can buy tortellini both fresh and dried from good supermarkets. They are tiny parcels of pasta usually stuffed with meat or a cheese and spinach mixture. Serve with ciabatta bread, a dish of olives and a mixed, dressed salad.

SERVES 4

INGREDIENTS	METRIC	IMPERIAL	AMERICAN
Tortellini (or other stuffed pasta shapes)	*250 g*	*9 oz*	*1 packet*
1 jar Italian tomato pasta sauce			
Parmesan cheese, grated			

METHOD

❶ Cook the pasta according to packet directions. Drain.

❷ Heat the pasta sauce in a fondue pot, stirring until heated through.

❸ Guests spear the tortellini, dip in the hot sauce, holding it in for a few seconds to heat through, then dip in Parmesan cheese before eating.

Preparation time: 10 minutes

CLEVER WAYS WITH A PACKET OF CHEESE FONDUE

Bought cheese fondues are very good and ideal for a spontaneous party. Here are some ideas for giving it an original twist.

Mexican Fondue

Add 1.5-2.5 ml/^{1}/$_4$-^{1}/$_2$ tsp chilli powder or 1 green chilli, seeded and finely chopped, to the fondue and serve with tortilla chips.

Indian Fondue

Add 5 ml/1 tsp curry paste to the fondue, and serve with pieces of naan bread, slices of banana and apple tossed in lemon juice.

Quick Tomato Fondue

Add 15 ml/1 tbsp tomato ketchup or purée (catsup or paste) or to taste. Serve with vegetable sticks and wholemeal bread.

Ham Fondue

Add 100 g/4 oz/1 cup finely diced cooked ham to the fondue.

Cucumber Fondue

Rub a cut garlic clove round the fondue pot before adding the cheese mixture, and add ^{1}/$_4$ cucumber, very finely diced, just before serving.

Crunchy Fondue

Add 50 g/2 oz/^{1}/$_2$ cup crispy onions or bacon topping, or tiny soup croûtons to the fondue before dipping.

Nutty Special

Add 50 g/2 oz/^{1}/$_2$ cup chopped walnuts to the fondue, and simmer for 2 minutes. Serve with celery sticks.

Dessert Fondues

Sweet, luxurious, exotic – the following fondues make the perfect end to any meal even if it wasn't a full-blown fondue party.

If you can't face actually *cooking* another fondue – serve bowls of soft fruits, whipped cream, liqueur and sugar for guests to dip into – the perfect chilled fondue!

Raspberry Meringue Fondue

Serve with a bowl of whipped cream or fromage frais.

SERVES 4

INGREDIENTS	METRIC	IMPERIAL	AMERICAN
Fresh or frozen raspberries,			
thawed	*350 g*	*12 oz*	*3 cups*
Icing (confectioner's sugar)	*15-30 ml*	*1 tbsp*	*1 tbsp*
Cornflour (cornstarch)	*10 ml*	*2 tsp*	*2 tsp*
Water	*30 ml*	*2 tbsp*	*2 tbsp*
Bite-sized meringues	*16*	*16*	*16*
Kiwi fruit, peeled and			
sliced	*2*	*2*	*2*

METHOD

❶ Purée the raspberries in a blender or processor then sieve into a fondue pot.

❷ Blend the sugar, cornflour and water together until smooth and stir in. Cook, stirring until thickened and bubbling. Taste and add more sugar if necessary.

❸ Arrange meringues and kiwi fruit on serving plates and serve.

Preparation time: 10 minutes

Chocolate Orange Fondue

Serve with profiteroles filled with whipped cream or cubes
of gingerbread and segments of satsumas or clementines.

SERVES 4

INGREDIENTS	METRIC	IMPERIAL	AMERICAN
Plain (semi-sweet)			
chocolate	*250 g*	*9 oz*	*9 oz*
Double (heavy) cream	*120 ml*	*4 fl oz*	*¹/₂ cup*
Grated rind of 1 orange			
Orange liqueur	*30 ml*	*2 tbsp*	*2 tbsp*

METHOD

❶ Break up the chocolate and place in a fondue pot with
the cream. Heat, stirring until the chocolate melts and
combines with the cream. Stir in the orange rind and
liqueur.

❷ Keep over a low heat, stirring frequently. Serve.

Preparation time: 10 minutes

Rum 'n' Butter Fondue

Other tropical fruits taste good with this fondue too.

SERVES 6

INGREDIENTS	METRIC	IMPERIAL	AMERICAN
Light brown sugar	*225 g*	*8 oz*	*1 cup*
Single (light) cream	*450 ml*	*³/₄ pt*	*2 cups*
Butter	*50 g*	*2 oz*	*¹/₄ cup*
Cornflour (cornstarch)	*40 g*	*1¹/₂ oz*	*¹/₃ cup*
Rum	*45 ml*	*3 tbsp*	*3 tbsp*
Bananas, cut in chunks	*6*	*6*	*6*
Lemon juice			
Small macaroons			

METHOD

❶ Heat the sugar, cream and butter in a fondue pot or a saucepan until melted, stirring all the time.

❷ Blend the cornflour with the rum and stir in. Bring to the boil, stirring until thickened. Transfer to a fondue pot, if necessary. Place on the table.

❸ Toss the bananas in lemon juice to prevent browning and arrange on plates with the macaroons. Serve.

Preparation time: 10 minutes

Sherry Trifle Fondue

Serve with a bowl of custard (canned is ideal), whipped cream and chopped, toasted nuts.

SERVES 4

INGREDIENTS	METRIC	IMPERIAL	AMERICAN
Icing (confectioner's sugar)	350 g	12 oz	2 cups
Butter, softened	100 g	4 oz	1/2 cup
Boiling water	120 ml	4 fl oz	1/2 cup
Medium sherry	175 ml	6 fl oz	3/4 cup
Trifle sponges, cut in cubes	4-6	4-6	4-6
Sliced strawberries (or other soft fruit)	225 g	8 oz	2 cups

METHOD

❶ Cream the icing sugar and butter together in a bowl. Beat in the boiling water. When smooth, stir in the sherry. Turn into a fondue pot and keep warm over a moderate heat.

❷ Arrange the trifle sponges and fruit on serving plates. Guests dip a piece of cake and fruit in the fondue until coated. Then eat with custard, cream and nuts.

Preparation time: 10 minutes

Peach Mallow Fondue

You definitely need a sweet tooth for this one!

SERVES 4

INGREDIENTS	METRIC	IMPERIAL	AMERICAN
Marshmallows	*100 g*	*4 oz*	*1 cup*
Icing (confectioner's) sugar	*30 ml*	*2 tbsp*	*2 tbsp*
Whipping cream	*150 ml*	*¼ pt*	*²/₃ cup*
Lemon juice	*15-30 ml*	*1-2 tbsp*	*1-2 tbsp*
Ripe peaches, peeled, stoned (pitted) and sliced	*4*	*4*	*4*
Packet sponge finger biscuits (ladies' fingers)	*1*	*1*	*1*

METHOD

❶ Snip the marshmallows with wet scissors into small pieces.

❷ Place in a fondue pot with the sugar and cream and heat gently, stirring until the marshmallows melt and blend with the sugar and cream. Do not allow to boil. Stir in the lemon juice.

❸ Keep over a very gentle heat, stirring frequently so the mixture doesn't catch.

❹ Arrange the peach slices and sponge fingers on serving plates and serve.

Preparation time: 10 minutes

Date and Apricot Fondue

Offer wedges of fresh lime to suck between mouthfuls.

SERVES 4

INGREDIENTS	METRIC	IMPERIAL	AMERICAN
Marshmallows	100 g	4 oz	1 cup
Evaporated milk	150 ml	$^1/_4$ pt	$^2/_3$ cup
Orange liqueur	15-30 ml	1-2 tbsp	1-2 tbsp
Fresh dates, stoned (pitted)	12	12	12
Fresh, ripe apricots, halved and stoned (pitted)	4 or 8	4 or 8	4 or 8

METHOD

1 Snip the marshmallows with wet scissors into pieces and place in a fondue pot with the evaporated milk. Heat gently, stirring until the marshmallows have melted. Stir in the liqueur to taste.

2 Keep over a low heat so the mixture doesn't catch, stirring frequently.

3 Arrange the dates and apricots on serving plates and serve.

Preparation time: 10 minutes

Speciality Coffee Fondue

The dessert and coffee course in one! Serve with individual dishes of whipped cream and grated chocolate.

SERVES 4

INGREDIENTS	METRIC	IMPERIAL	AMERICAN
Mini ring doughnuts, or tiny			
dropped scones	*6*	*6*	*6*
Strong black coffee	*900 ml*	*1¹/₂ pts*	*3³/₄ cups*
Brandy or whisky	*45 ml*	*3 tbsp*	*3 tbsp*
Light brown sugar	*15 ml*	*1 tbsp*	*1 tbsp*

METHOD

❶ Arrange the doughnuts or dropped scones on serving plates.

❷ Heat the coffee, brandy and sugar in a fondue pot until piping hot, stirring until the sugar has dissolved.

❸ Guests dip the doughnuts or dropped scones in the coffee then in cream and chocolate. When all the doughnuts have been dunked, strain the coffee into small cups and serve.

Preparation time: 10 minutes

Maple Fondue

Sweet, sickly and wonderfully light, this fondue should be served warm with fresh strawberries or waffles, cut in cubes.

SERVES 6–8

INGREDIENTS	METRIC	IMPERIAL	AMERICAN
Milk	450 ml	³/₄ pt	2 cups
Pinch of salt			
Egg yolks	5	5	5
Maple syrup	150 ml	¹/₄ pt	²/₃ cup
Brandy	30 ml	2 tbsp	2 tbsp
Single (light) cream	75 ml	5 tbsp	5 tbsp

METHOD

1 Heat the milk with the salt. Beat the egg yolks together and add to the milk, whisking.

2 Gradually stir in the maple syrup and cook gently until the custard thickens and coats the back of a spoon.

3 Stir in the brandy and cream. Transfer to a fondue pot, keeping the flame very low.

Preparation time: 10 minutes

Coconut Fondue

Serve with cubes of gingerbread, banana tossed in lemon juice and any other tropical fruits of your choice.

SERVES 4

INGREDIENTS	METRIC	IMPERIAL	AMERICAN
Desiccated (shredded)			
coconut	*100 g*	*4 oz*	*1 cup*
Creamed coconut, chopped	*75 g*	*3 oz*	*³/₄ cup*
Caster (superfine) sugar	*50 g*	*2 oz*	*¹/₄ cup*
Cornflour (cornstarch)	*20 ml*	*4 tsp*	*4 tsp*
Single (light) cream	*150 ml*	*¹/₄ pt*	*²/₃ cup*

METHOD

❶ Put the desiccated coconut in a saucepan with 600 ml/ 1 pt/2 ¹/₂ cups water, the creamed coconut and the sugar. Bring to the boil and simmer for 15 minutes. Strain the mixture through a fine sieve (strainer) to extract all the liquid.

❷ Blend the cornflour with the cream until smooth and add to the coconut liquid.

❸ Pour into a fondue pot and cook gently, stirring, until the mixture thickens. Serve warm, not hot.

Preparation time: 20 minutes

Chilled Champagne Fondue

Serve with strawberries or a selection of soft fruits.

SERVES 4–6

INGREDIENTS	METRIC	IMPERIAL	AMERICAN
Eggs	3	3	3
Caster (superfine) sugar	50 g	2 oz	1/4 cup
Finely grated rind of 1 orange			
Double (heavy) cream	150 ml	1/4 pt	2/3 cup
Champagne or sparkling wine	150 ml	1/4 pt	2/3 cup
Single (light) cream	150 ml	1/4 pt	2/3 cup

METHOD

❶ Put the eggs, sugar and orange rind in a bowl. Stand the bowl over a saucepan of hot water and whisk until the mixture is thick and fluffy.

❷ Remove the bowl from the saucepan and whisk in the double cream.

❸ Stir in the Champagne and single cream and whisk until blended. Serve chilled.

Preparation time: 10 minutes

Black Cherry Fondue

Serve with cubes of chocolate or almond cake.

SERVES 4–6

INGREDIENTS	METRIC	IMPERIAL	AMERICAN
Granulated sugar	30 ml	2 tbsp	2 tbsp
Black cherries, stoned			
(pitted)	1 kg	2^1/$_4$ lb	9 cups
Red wine	150 ml	^{1}/$_4$ pt	^{2}/$_3$ cup
Cinnamon	5 ml	1 tsp	1 tsp
Grated nutmeg	5 ml	1 tsp	1 tsp

METHOD

❶ Put all the ingredients into a saucepan and simmer for 15 minutes. Purée in a blender or food processor. Pour into a fondue pot on a low heat. Serve.

Preparation time: 20 minutes

White Chocolate Fondue

You can, of course, substitute dark chocolate if you prefer. Serve with shortbread fingers and cubes of coconut ice.

SERVES 4

INGREDIENTS	METRIC	IMPERIAL	AMERICAN
White chocolate squares	175 g	6 oz	1 cup
Single (light) cream	250 ml	8 fl oz	1 cup
Icing (confectioner's) sugar	100 g	4 oz	^{2}/$_3$ cup
Butter	50 g	2 oz	^{1}/$_4$ cup
Vanilla essence (extract)	5 ml	1 tsp	1 tsp

METHOD

❶ Put all the ingredients except the vanilla into a fondue pot. Heat gently, stirring all the time until melted and blended. Add the vanilla.

❷ Keep over a low heat, stirring frequently for a few minutes until thickened then serve.

Preparation time: 10 minutes

Simple Chocolate Fondue

Serve with cubes of plain cake, fresh soft fruits or marshmallows and whole nuts like Brazils or walnuts.

SERVES 6

INGREDIENTS	METRIC	IMPERIAL	AMERICAN
Chocolate chips	350 g	12 oz	3 cups
Powdered milk (non-fat dry milk)	40 g	1¹/₂ oz	¹/₃ cup
Boiling water	120 ml	4 fl oz	¹/₂ cup
Vanilla essence (extract)	5 ml	1 tsp	1 tsp

METHOD

❶ Put the chocolate in a fondue pot. Whisk the milk and water together and add to the pot with the vanilla. Heat gently, stirring all the time, until thickened and melted. Do not boil.

❷ Reduce heat to low and stir frequently to prevent catching. Serve.

Preparation time: 10 minutes

ale batter fondue 50-51
anchovies
    bagna cauda 30
apricot fondue, date and 150
artichokes
    crab stick and artichoke fondue 44
    new potatoes and artichoke fondue
      113

bacon
    gourmet fondue 68
    metze fondue 91
    see also gammon
bagna cauda 30-31
bananas
    rum'n'butter fondue 147
bean and sweetcorn fondue 110-11
beef
    meatball fondue 54-5
    see also steak
Belgian fondue 12-13
Bianco fondue 24
birds of a feather fondue 60-61
black cherry fondue 155
black-eyed beans
    bean and sweetcorn fondue 110-11
blushing mixed fondue 83
bouillabaisse fondue 43
Bretonne fondue 42

Caerphilly fondue 23
calvados, Camembert and 14
Caribbean fondue 45
caviar sauce 123
champagne
    chilled champagne fondue 154
    creamy champagne and seafood
      fondue 38-9
cheat sauces 137
cheese
    Belgian fondue 12-13
    Bianco fondue 24
    Caerphilly fondue 23
    Camembert and calvados 14
    cheese and onion sauce 137
    cheese and vegetable fondue 27
    crunchy fondue 143
    cucumber fondue 143
    curried fondue 16
    Dutch fondue 25
    fondue Italienne 15

golden Camemberts 18-19
ham fondue 143
Indian fondue 143
Italian pizza fondue 22
Mexican fondue 143
nutty special 143
ploughman's fondue 21
quick tomato fondue 143
rich Geneva convention 26
a romantic fondue 20-21
simple Gruyère fondue 13
Swiss fondue 17
Worcestershire fondue 19
chick peas
    spicy cumin balls 108
chicken
    ale batter fondue 50-51
    birds of a feather fondue 60-61
    Caribbean fondue 45
    cheesy cream fondue 86
    chicken Maryland fondue 141
    Chinese complete creation 92-3
    Chinese noodle fondue 72
    country fondue 67
    fondue bourguignon 57
    fondue hotpot 71
    Greek fondue 62-3
    herb fondue 80
    Indian extravaganza 94
    Indonesian kebab fondue 96-7
Chinese complete creation 92-3
Chinese garlic sauce 126
Chinese noodle fondue 72
Chinese wire strainers 18, 31
chocolate
    chocolate orange fondue 146
    simple chocolate fondue 156
    white chocolate fondue 155-6
chop suey fondue 100-101
Christmas fondue 106
cocktail sauce 122
coconut fondue 153
coffee fondue, speciality 151
Cornish crab fondue 39
country fondue 67
crab
    Cornish crab fondue 39
    crab stick and artichoke fondue 44
cranberry relish 133
cucumber and mint sauce 136
cucumber fondue 143

cumin balls, spicy 108
curry sauce, hot 130
curried fondue 16

date and apricot fondue 150
dill cream 124
doughnuts
    speciality coffee fondue 151
drinks 9
duck
    birds of a feather fondue 60-61
    chop suey fondue 100-101
    crispy duck with pepper sauce 56-7
    fondue for kings 79
    Indonesian kebab fondue 96-7
    Mongolian munch 104-5
Dutch fondue 25

equipment 5

farmer's fondue 48-9
fiery lamb fondue 64
filo parcels, filled 32-3
fines herbes sauce 127
fondue bourguignon 57
fondue cookery 4, 5-7, 8-10, 46, 69
    cheese fondues 6, 8
    equipment 5
    fish fondues 6-7, 8-9
    meat fondues 6-7, 8-9
    procedure 8-9
    secrets of success 10
    sweet fondues 7, 9
    vegetable fondues 6-7, 8-9
fondue for connoisseurs 95
fondue for kings 79
fondue hotpot 71
fondue Italienne 15
fonduta di Napoli 84-5
forester's fondue 82
frito misto di mare fondue 40-41

gammon
    creamy champagne and seafood
        fondue 38-9
    fonduta di Napoli 84-5
    forester's fondue 82
    gammon plus fondue 78
garden fondue 87

garlic
    Chinese garlic sauce 126
    garlic sauce 131
ginger sauce 135
golden Camemberts 18-19
goose
    fondue for kings 79
    Mongolian munch 104-5
gourmet fondue 68
Greek fondue 62-3

ham
    gammon plus fondue 78
    ham fondue 143
hare
    fondue for connoisseurs 95
herbs
    fines herbes sauce 127
    herb cream 125
    herb fondue 80
    herby potato balls 109
    see also individual types e.g. dill
Hong Kong Hilton! 102-3
hot curry sauce 130
hot dog fondue 140

Indian extravaganza 94
Indian fondue 143
Indonesian kebab fondue 96-7
Italian pizza fondue 22

kebabs
    Indonesian kebab fondue 96-7
    vegetarian kebab fondue 112
Kievs, mini
    Russian fondue 139

lamb
    crispy speciality fondue 98-9
    fiery lamb fondue 64
    fondue bourguignon 57
    fondue for connoisseurs 95
    fondue hotpot 71
    gourmet fondue 68
    Greek fondue 62-3
    Indian extravaganza 94
    minted lamb fondue 51
    rustic fondue 65
    sparkling French fondue 81
    sweet and sour fondue 74-5
    Welsh lamb fondue 73

lambs' kidneys
 chop suey fondue 100-101
lambs' liver
 cheesy cream fondue 86
 chop suey fondue 100-101
lobster
 Indonesian kebab fondue 96-7
 witch's fondue 88-9

maple fondue 152
marinated pork fondue 58
marshmallow
 date and apricot fondue 150
 peach mallow fondue 149
meatball fondue 54-5
meringue fondue, raspberry 145
metze fondue 91
Mexican fondue 143
mint
 cucumber and mint sauce 136
 minted lamb fondue 51
mixed sausage fondue 55
Mongolian munch 104-5
mushrooms
 crispy fried mushrooms 116
 mushroom fondue 111
mustard sauce 129

new potatoes and artichoke fondue
  113
noodle fondue, Chinese 72
nutty special 143

oil, cooking in 6, 46
onion sauce, cheese and 137
Oriental beef fondue 69

peach mallow fondue 149
peppercorn sauce 128
peppers
 crispy duck with pepper sauce 56-
  7
 red pepper sauce 132
pheasant
 birds of a feather fondue 60-61
pigs' liver
 Hong Kong Hilton! 102-3
pimiento fondue 117
pineapple
 sweet and sour sauce 120
 whipped pineapple sauce 119

plaice
 Caribbean fondue 45
 plaice goujons 34
ploughman's fondue 21
pork
 ale batter fondue 50-51
 blushing mixed fondue 83
 cheesy cream fondue 86
 Chinese complete creation 92-3
 crispy speciality fondue 98-9
 farmer's fondue 48-9
 fondue bourguignon 57
 forester's fondue 82
 gammon plus fondue 78
 gourmet fondue 68
 Hong Kong Hilton! 102-3
 Indonesian kebab fondue 96-7
 marinated pork fondue 58
 meatball fondue 54-5
 Mongolian munch 104-5
 pork and vegetable fondue 66
 pork satay 49
 Russian fondue 139
 sweet and sour fondue 74-5
 Trieste fondue 70
 witch's fondue 88-9
potatoes
 herby potato balls 109
 new potatoes and artichoke fondue
  113
 potato skins 115
prawns
 Bretonne fondue 42
 filled filo parcels 32-3
 spicy prawns 33

rabbit
 herb fondue 80
raspberry meringue fondue 145
ravioli
 fonduta di Napoli 84-5
rich Geneva convention 26
romantic fondue 20-21
rouille 121
rum'n'butter fondue 147
Russian fondue 139
rustic fondue 65

sausages and sausagemeat
 hot dog fondue 140
 mixed sausage fondue 55

Russian fondue 139
rustic fondue 65
sausage savouries 47
supper sausage fondue 76-7
sweet and sour fondue 74-5
seafood
  creamy champagne and seafood
    fondue 38-9
  seafood fondue 29
shellfish
  bouillabaisse fondue 43
  Bretonne fondue 42
  seafood fondue 29
  see also prawns
sherry trifle fondue 148
sole and sherry fondue 31
spare ribs
  Chinese complete creation 92-3
  farmer's fondue 48-9
sparkling French fondue 81
speciality coffee fondue 151
spicy cumin balls 108
spicy prawns 33
squid
  metze fondue 91
steak
  beef steak fondue 59
  blushing mixed fondue 83
  chop suey fondue 100-101
  creamy champagne and seafood
    fondue 38-9
  crispy speciality fondue 98-9
  fondue bourguignon 57
  fonduta di Napoli 84-5
  garden fondue 87
  gourmet fondue 68
  Oriental beef fondue 69
  sparkling French fondue 81
  surf'n'turf fondue 36-7
  too-hot-to-handle steak 52-3
  witch's fondue 88-9
supper sausage fondue 76-7
surf'n'turf fondue 36-7
sweet and sour fondue 74-5
sweet and sour sauce 120
sweet spicy sauce 134
sweetcorn fondue, bean and 110-11
Swiss fondue 17

tofu
  garden fondue 87

pork and vegetable fondue 66
tomato fondue, vegetable and 114-15
too-hot-to-handle steak 52-3
tortellini fondue 142
Trieste fondue 70
turkey
  blushing mixed fondue 83
  Chinese noodle fondue 72
  Christmas fondue 106
  country fondue 67
  fondue for kings 79

veal
  Bretonne fondue 42
  chop suey fondue 100-101
  fondue for kings 79
  witch's fondue 88-9
vegetables
  cheese and vegetable fondue 27
  pork and vegetable fondue 66
  vegetable and tomato fondue 114-
    15
  vegetable kebab fondue 112
  see also individual types e.g.
    potatoes
venison
  fondue for kings 79
  forester's fondue 82
  sparkling French fondue 81

Welsh lamb fondue 73
whipped pineapple sauce 119
witch's fondue 88-9
Worcestershire fondue 19